Rod Paschall

A PERIGEE BOOK

The photographs appearing on pages
49, 105, and 121 are from the U.S. Air Force;
the photograph appearing on page 43
is from the U.S. Marines;
all other photographs and maps
are from the U.S. Army.

A Perigee Book
Published by The Berkley Publishing Group
200 Madison Avenue
New York, NY 10016

First edition: June 1995

Published simultaneously in Canada.

Library of Congress Cataloging-in-Publication Data
Paschall, Rod.
Witness to war : Korea / Rod Paschall.—1st ed.
p.   cm.
"A Perigee book".
ISBN 0-399-51934-3
1. Korean War, 1950–1953—Personal narratives, American.
2. Korean War, 1950–1953—Participation, American.   I. Title.
DS921.6.P33   1995
951.904′2—dc20   94-39653
                                          CIP

Printed in the United States of America

10   9   8   7   6   5   4   3   2

FOR SAM

CONTENTS

PHOTOGRAPHS
AND MAPS

Photographs

Maps

PREFACE

I GREW UP with the Korean War. When I was fourteen, a carefree summer vacation was interrupted by the dramatic radio announcement of North Korea's invasion of the South. Like most Americans, I had no idea where the two Koreas were. But my older brother, Sam, showed me a map, and pointed out the location of that Asian peninsula. Sam had more than a casual interest in Korea. He was draft age. Within a few months, he had completed basic training and I was able to visit him, getting my first look at the U.S. Army. To me, raised in a small Texas cow town, it was a grand, important, and righteous adventure—heady stuff. Because of Sam and Korea, I was forever hooked on being a soldier.

The war was over by the time I graduated from high school and won an appointment to West Point, but I found that almost all my instructors at the Academy were fresh from Korea. My undergraduate education was therefore heavily salted with stories from that war. When I was cutting my eyeteeth as a paratroop platoon leader in the 187th Airborne Infantry, it was much the same. The sergeants and my superior officers, those who had the arduous duty of tutoring a neophyte second lieutenant, were all Korean War veterans—more stories. Later, when I joined Special Forces, I drew a field instructor who had been in a little-known unit in Korea, an outfit that trained and directed North Korean guerrillas to conduct raids behind Communist lines. Major John Farrell would observe our practices, usually nighttime ambushes and such, then gather us around a campfire for a critique. After pointing out the mistakes we had made, Farrell, with our enthusiastic encouragement, would tell us what it had been like in Korea with the guerrillas.

By the time I got to Korea, in 1965, I had two Southeast Asian combat tours under my belt and believed I knew just about everything there was to know about fighting. But I quickly discovered how much I had to learn. I was a company commander in the 32nd Infantry, a unit that would immediately counterattack if the North Koreans came across the Demilitarized Zone. There were some seven U.S. counterattack plans scattered around the western part of the Peninsula and we had to know the ground for each of them. To ensure we knew our parts, our battalion commander, Lieutenant Colonel Carroll D. Shealey, took his company commanders to each of these spots. There, we would walk the planned counterattack corridors. Duty done, Shealey would lead us to a special place, one that he had fought at during the war. More stories were unfolded: what tactics the Chinese had used, the way they defended a hill. He gave us a firsthand account of how the North Koreans had used their weapons, their night attack techniques, and the likely positions they would use for their command posts. Shealey would tell us what had worked and what had failed from the American point of view. Then he would quiz us. What would we do? How would we position our weapons? Although I had led units in combat in Vietnam and had graduated from both the Infantry and Armor Schools, I really learned my profession in Korea.

Returning to Vietnam in 1966, I took command of a rifle company in the 27th Infantry (nicknamed the Wolfhounds) and plunged into a much bigger war than the one I had known a few years before. During the next six months, the 27th Infantry took a fearsome toll on the Viet Cong and North Vietnamese. We suffered losses as well. In my company, there would be ninety men wounded, including myself. But there was only one man killed. By any measure, it was a good record, one I attribute to my experience—and to what I had learned on those hills in Korea. In more ways than one, the Korean War had been my school and there are undoubtedly a number of Americans alive today because of it.

ACKNOWLEDGMENTS

I ENJOYED THE support and assistance of many good people in writing this book. At the Military History Institute in Carlisle, Pennsylvania, John Slonaker, Denis Vetock, Judy Provins, Louise Friend, and Kathleen Gildersleeve helped me find books and documents. Dr. Richard Sommers, David Keough, and Pam Cheney helped me with manuscripts, oral histories, and personal papers. Michael Winey and Randy Hackenburg pointed me to the right photos. And at Putnam, my editor, Julie Merberg, asked all the right questions and suggested all the right changes.

I would be remiss if I did not thank all those who helped me understand the Korean War. In addition to Major John Farrell and Lieutenant Colonel Carroll D. Shealey, there was Sergeant Roberto Vasquez and Captain (later Major General) George Marine. For the war in the air, a veteran B-26 pilot, Colonel Jim Enos, not only told me a few tales about interdiction, he worked some highly professional magic in reproducing forty year old photographs for this book. During the 1980s I was a guest in the home of General Matthew B. Ridgway on several occasions and learned much about the war from that great and well-

respected soldier. Earlier still, in the mid-1960s, I had the good
fortune to work closely with Lieutenant General Frederick
Carleton Weyand, who had been a battalion commander during
the Korean War. Weyand shared a few of his stories and observations and I was delighted to find a description of one of his
encounters with the Chinese, a story that is retold in these
pages. Colonel Robert J. Gerard was kind enough to spend a
day recording the sensations, scenes, and sounds of the war's
last day. Most of all, thanks to my brother, Sam.

                              Rod Paschall
                              Carlisle, Pennsylvania
                              August 1994

INTRODUCTION

THIS STORY OF the Korean War is mostly told by those who witnessed it—Americans, Chinese, North Koreans—whoever had something profound, revealing, or important to say. The quotations here are usually those made at the time the war was going on. Fundamentally, it is a contemporary account. You'll find the words of diplomats, generals, pilots, presidents, captains, sergeants, privates, admirals, and most of all, foot soldiers. More than any others, the infantrymen of both sides shaped the outcome. It was that kind of sweat, mud, bone, leather, blood, and cold steel armed conflict. It was also a war where uniformed American historians often recorded participants' stories immediately after an action. There are a number of these vividly captured tales in this book. There are also some experiences from support troops and logisticians. No record of a war would ever be complete without the views of those who supplied and assisted frontline fighters. The source of each quoted section will be found in the notes following the last chapter. There has been a conscious effort to keep the author's connecting narrative and conclusions to a minimum. The spotlight, as much as possible, is on the warmakers and witnesses.

This war is one of America's least analyzed and therefore least understood. There are sound reasons for the lack of previous attention to the Korean conflict. Normally, historians begin the first light survey histories of a conflict about a decade after the event. But it is not until all the major participants have written their memoirs and government archives are opened, usually thirty years after the war, that comprehensive histories can be attempted. In the case of the Korean War, the flood of Civil War centennial literature was crowding other books off the stands ten years after the Korean cease-fire. And thirty years after that cease-fire, the outpouring of World War II books was still continuing. Then, too, the Korean War was wedged between the Second World War and the Vietnam War, two huge American episodes that have overshadowed the intervening conflict.

There are good books about the war, but many were written with considerable attention paid to events in the making or with an eye to justifying wartime decisions. One of the Korean War's greatest legacies was that it shaped much of the Cold War, and any author writing in the 1960s, 1970s, or early 1980s could not foresee the middle or end of the larger struggle. In that era, writers could only see the Cold War's beginnings. Therefore, the Korean War could not be placed into historical perspective until the early 1990s, after the collapse of Communism, the triumph of the West, and the Cold War's end.

Now that it is possible to place the Korean War in context, it is certainly appropriate to do so. Suddenly, there are tens of thousands of troops serving under the United Nations banner throughout the world, and it is timely to reflect on the first war the U.N. fought. Now, despite the fact that the U.S. Central Intelligence Agency has not fully opened its Korean War archives, it is quite possible to learn why the United States government was so badly informed about North Korea during 1949 and 1950. Now, since the Department of Defense has removed the wraps of secrecy from its partisan operations files from the 1950s, it is possible to tell the story of the several thousand North Koreans who, under American direction, operated behind Chinese and North Korean lines during the war.

Being mainly a witnesses' account, this book is neither a definitive history of the war nor a standard, third-person narrative history. As much as possible, the firsthand thoughts and experiences are those recorded as the war was being waged, not those that occurred to someone years later. In some cases, contemporary statements about some important events or issues were not recorded, so later reflections are used. However, the bias of these pages is for the fresh recollections, aspirations, fears, and excitement of the early 1950s. In the last chapter, there is hindsight. There, the quest is to answer a simple question, one that was often posed during the war: was the Korean War the wrong war, at the wrong time, at the wrong place? It was a good question then and perhaps a better one today.

There have been changes in some of the quoted text. Military-style dates and times have been replaced by versions in general use. During the war the island-nation of Taiwan and its inhabitants played a tangential role, but at the time, the island was known as Formosa, not Taiwan, and to avoid possible confusion, the island's current name is used. Parentheses within the quotations of the text were there in the 1950s version, including interpolations made by the original editors or authors. In cases where an explanation seemed necessary, the author has supplied notes in brackets. The author has also supplied short, connecting narratives to ensure the reader is in step with the war's progress. Other than these exceptions, the reader will find words here as they were written and spoken during those grim days in the early 1950s. Mostly, this story is told by those who made it.

KOREA

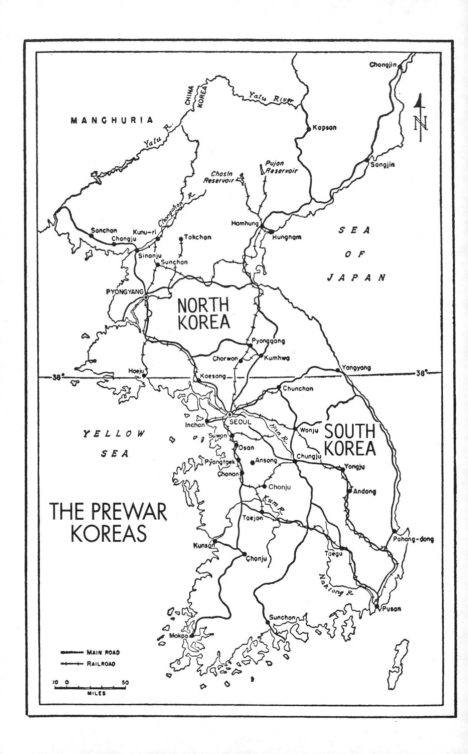

THE PREWAR KOREAS

WRONG PLACE, WRONG TIME, WRONG WAR

KOREA, JANUARY 12, 1951. In a cold, drafty tent, not far from the front lines, fourteen Americans huddled around an oil heater. One was older, over fifty, a U.S. Army historian and veteran of both world wars. Sent down from higher headquarters, he would conduct a routine after-action interview. The others, mostly in their twenties, were members of E Company, 27th Infantry, the regiment known to most American foot soldiers as the Wolfhounds. There was the company commander, Captain Louis L. Millett, two of his lieutenants, three sergeants, three corporals, and four privates. As artillery fire boomed in the distance, trucks and jeeps rumbled by outside. Despite the chilly wind piercing the canvas, the men, hesitant at first and only responding to the historian's questions, grew attentive, intense, and soon needed no prompting. For the old-timer, they eagerly reconstructed just what happened only five days ago:

CAPTAIN MILLETT: I saw Cockrell and a group of about fifteen of his men. They were in an irrigation ditch off the flank of the hill and on the left of our general position. I had to yell to Cockrell as I came into his line.

SERGEANT FLOYD E. COCKRELL: He said, "Get ready to move. We're going to assault the hill. Fix bayonets! When I yell, Charge!—everybody goes." It was seventy-five yards to the base of the hill. There was no cover—just frozen rice paddies. From the moment we started, small arms fire came against us.

MILLETT: We charged to the base of the hill. Then I turned to see how the men were moving up.

COCKRELL: I would say that we weren't doing too well at that moment, when we got to the base of the hill there were only fourteen of us present.

MILLETT: I figured we did pretty well to get that many men forward under those circumstances. I kept right on moving from the base of the hill and up the slope. The fourteen men were moving right along with me. The CCF [Chinese Communist Forces] machine gun on the left of their hill position was hitting hard into the others who were still crossing the paddy fields behind us. I saw several of them get hit and fall on the ice, and looking back, I could see the bullets splintering the ice among them. I knew that fire had to be stopped if we were to get the needed support to us.

   Third platoon came charging right across the little valley. But it was a strange charge and an even worse start. I didn't realize how icy the slope of that hill was they were holding until I saw them try to take off and come at us on the run. Then I witnessed some of my men in this platoon pitch headlong as they cleared the summit and coasted down the hill as if they were toboggans. But somehow most of them managed to hold on to their weapons. When they got to the bottom, they were still confronted by solid ice; between them and our hill there existed nothing but a series of completely ice-covered rice paddies. They came on at a dead run, yelling like fiends out of Hell. They had to run fifty yards down the snow-covered slope and an additional hundred yards across the flat—this in the face of enemy fire. Those who had fallen picked themselves up immediately and kept on coming. I didn't see a single man lag behind. The line of their advance brought 3rd Platoon in on our right, half way up the hill.

CORPORAL HERBERT FAULKNER: I was with 3rd Platoon during its charge. Burp guns over on our right flank and half way up the hill, a machine gun, backed up by riflemen, were pouring a hail of bullets at us. It splintered the ice all around and began hitting among the men. PFC Howard Baumgardner had one slug cut his BAR [Browning automatic rifle] sling and another knock out the rear sight. It hit so hard that it knocked him down. He picked himself up and kept running toward the hill, though he was now weaponless. Then a piece of metal, I think from a mortar, hit him in the leg. A bullet tore away part of his pants. He went down again, picked himself up and kept on charging toward the hill. We had decided to carry our machine gun during the charge. PFC John Lescallet was carrying it, and he still doesn't know how he managed to get down that icy slope with it at a run. First, his bipod was shot away. Then a bullet hit the machine gun right over the cover latch and ruined it. So he threw the gun away. Lescallet kept on going, using his pistol until it was empty and then using hand grenades.

MILLETT: Third platoon, coming abreast of us, tied in on the right. I walked about twenty feet over to them and told Lammond to attack straight up the hill.

LIEUTENANT JOHN T. LAMMOND: The captain, after giving me the order, ran straight back up the hill to the hole which I had previously grenaded, because we were continuing to get grenades from this same ground. As he gave me the order to advance to the crest, I yelled over to Brockmier. But as things turned out, the order was unnecessary. The men had already taken the situation into their own hands and were continuing to move up the hill without any order.

SERGEANT DONALD BROCKMIER: The truth is we had not even paused when we came to the base of the hill. After crossing the flat, my men kept right on going. . . . We were grenading as we advanced. . . . Lescallet, Corporal Marshal Fletcher, Corporal Joseph Cyr, Sergeant Robert Blair and myself. . . . (All of these men except Brockmier were later killed in this same action.)

LAMMOND: Captain Millett ran up the slope. I saw him get within ten feet of a foxhole. Then the enemy threw another grenade.

FAULKNER: I was about ten yards to the captain's left as he came up to the foxhole. This put me within fifteen feet of the enemy position. But I couldn't do anything about it. You see, it was this way: one of the Gooks poked a gun out of this hole and was firing directly on me, at a range of only fifteen feet, and I was trying to duck back and forth to avoid the fire. . . . I yelled over to the captain: "Get them if you can, I can't."

MILLETT: . . . I didn't hear Faulkner. . . . Stuff was exploding all around me. Nine grenades fell right around me, three of which failed to explode. The last one threw a splinter of steel into my back. I saw the gun sticking out of the hole . . . I worked over to the reverse crest and came in on the left flank . . . I got within five feet and opened up on them with my M1.

PRIVATE CARMEN NUNNO: I saw Captain Millett go directly at one of these men with his bayonet, and I saw the bayonet enter his throat and go through his neck. Then the captain shot him to release his weapon. I tried to fire my M1 at the other Chinese. But my rifle just clicked and didn't fire. I saw one enemy stoop low and try to crawl back into a recess leading away from the foxhole. Three times I tried to bayonet him. But every time I lunged the blade slipped off the thick clothing he wore. It just wouldn't go in. On the fourth try I sunk it in between his shoulder blades and the thrust killed him.

MILLETT: I had bayoneted a second man, also in the throat, at this first foxhole. Nunno had killed a third enemy whom I had wholly overlooked in the excitement of the moment.

COCKRELL: . . . I got my bayonet into a Chinese in a foxhole. The thrust was downward into his neck and chest cavity. The blood spurted into my face. I wasn't sure that I had killed him so I fired my weapon. There was another enemy behind him. He looked at me but made no move to surrender. I shot him square between the eyes at the range of one foot.

NUNNO: Then over to the left I saw another foxhole with a Chinese in it. He was huddled, trying to hide himself or keep out of fire. With Private Harold Blodgett, my BAR man, looking on, I bayoneted him. He tried to stand up at the last minute and I got it through his chest. Two men popped their heads out of a foxhole just as I pulled the blade out. Blodgett saw them and he blew their heads off with his BAR. The captain was yelling at the top of his voice, "This is the way to take a goddamned hill! Now that you have this goddamned hill, hold it!"

As the bitter wind from Manchuria continued to howl, the men finished the story. The battle-seasoned historian checked over his notes, asking a few final questions. The interview was over. They all shuffled out into the cold. No one had thought to record the irony of it all. America, the richest and most technologically advanced nation on earth, possessed nuclear weapons and a continent-straddling fleet of bombers to deliver them. The United States Navy was so powerful it outranked all the world's navies combined. American jet fighters were daily proving superior to the best the Communist world could offer. Yet when

Fire, bayonet, and a Wolfhound. A member of the 27th Infantry fights his way north against Chinese forces, five miles southwest of Seoul, February 1951. The Regiment gained its nickname from its mascot, a Russian wolfhound, while it was in Manchuria in 1919.

this wealthy, industrial, scientific giant chose to go to war, its leaders threw the country's advantages aside. They decided on a foot soldier's fight—the most primitive form of war. Above all else, American success or failure in the Korean War hinged on the organization the country least prized and had least nurtured—its infantry.

At the very moment this and other after-action interviews were taking place in Korea, newspapers and magazines in the United States were full of tales about what U.S. riflemen had to face: crazed Chinese and North Korean human wave attacks.

Journalists and editors daily concluded that the callous governments of the two Communist countries simply did not care about their soldiers' lives. However, if some of the lucky Chinese who had managed to escape the brutal Wolfhound charge had been interviewed, they would have likely claimed it was the reckless, screaming, bayonet-wielding Americans who used human wave tactics.

How had it come about? What drove Americans to do this in a distant, godforsaken land few had heard of only one year before? What was it that made Americans suffer the same kind of attacks from their enemies, day after day and month after month for three years? In October 1952, while the war was still grinding on, the American Secretary of State, Dean G. Acheson, attempted to answer that question during a talk in New York City. The urbane, carefully dressed diplomat began his explanation with an event that had happened in Cairo, Egypt, in the midst of World War II, on the first day of December 1943:

"At that time, the representatives of China, the United States and the United Kingdom pledged themselves as being determined that, in due course, Korea should become free and independent. That pledge at Cairo was repeated by the same three powers at Potsdam [Germany] on 26 July 1945. There, it was agreed that the terms of the Cairo Declaration should be carried out. And upon its entry into the war against Japan, the Soviet Union adhered to the Potsdam Declaration, stating on 8 August 1945— and these words were the words used by the Soviet Government—'Loyal to its Allied duty, the Soviet Government has accepted the proposal of the Allies and has joined in the Declaration of the Allied Powers of 26 July.'

"This pledge was reaffirmed at Moscow on 27 December 1945. At that time, the Foreign Ministers of the United States, the United Kingdom and the Soviet Union agreed that a provisional Korean democratic government should be set up for all Korea with a view to the re-establishment of Korea as an independent state. Those were the promises. Those are the principles accepted by the Governments of China, the United States, the United Kingdom and the Soviet Union; namely, that Korea should be united, free and independent."

Secretary Acheson's explanation did not include circumstances that would have been elementary to his listeners in 1952. He did not mention the fact that during much of the early part of the twentieth century, Korea had been occupied by the Japanese Army, and that upon winning World War II, the Allies were anxious to set free all that Imperial Japan had conquered. The Secretary passed over the fact that the government of China that had signed these Allied agreements of the 1940s had been overthrown by Mao Tse-tung's Communist forces in 1949 and no longer supported the earlier pronouncements. At the time of this talk in New York, and for two more decades, the United States did not recognize the actual government on mainland China. Washington only dealt with Chiang Kai-shek's defeated regime-in-exile, the Chinese government on the island of Taiwan. Acheson did refer to the occupation of the Korean Peninsula by U.S. and Soviet troops and the agreed-upon geographical division between the two military occupation zones, the 38th parallel, and he went on to explain the mechanisms the two powers agreed to use in the Moscow Agreement of December 1945:

". . . one was a Joint Commission of the United States and the Soviet Union; and the other was the Joint Conference of the two powers. The Joint Commission was set up to

August 16, 1945. Soviets offer no objection to President Truman's proposal that the 38th Parallel divide U.S. and Soviet occupation zones in Korea. . . . .

South Korean political delegates seeking recognition in Seoul, October 1945.

work out the long-range political and economic problems, including the establishment of a provisional democratic structure for all of Korea. . . . The Joint Conference, on the other hand, was set up to deal with immediate and pressing questions. These had to do with the administrative and economic problems then existing in Korea. It was thought that by the joint efforts of the military authorities of the United States and the Soviet Union, these pressing, immediate economic and administrative questions could be solved.

"The Joint Conference met in January 1946 and the

. . . **January 9, 1946.** U.S. Joint Chiefs of Staff approve MacArthur's plans to create a lightly armed 50,000-man South Korean police force. . . . .

United States proposed a series of measures to advance the economic and administrative coordination of all Korea. These were very practical, possible and important steps. They were to unite the key public utilities, something that obviously should be done in a country which was about to be unified; and to create uniform fiscal policies, obviously very necessary to provide for the free flow of commodities back and forth throughout Korea. All of these proposals were rejected by the Soviet Union."

With a stalemate within the Joint Conference, the on-the-spot organization meant to deal with immediate problems, resolution had to be sought at a higher level. The Joint Commission, therefore, became the forum for the two powers, the United States and the Soviet Union, to work out their differences. The Commission had to agree on how to create a democracy in a nation that had never experienced representative government, how to unify the country, and how and when to withdraw all foreign forces so that Korea would stand whole, independent, and free. The 1945 Moscow Agreement had specified that the Commission would consult with Korean social and political groups during its deliberations. It soon became clear that the Soviets would not agree to the Commission consulting with some Korean groups. But there was something more. Excerpts from letters sent back and forth between Soviet and American officers during 1946 and 1947 revealed that the two governments could not agree on the meaning of an important word—*democracy*.

Letter from Lieutenant General John R. Hodge, Commanding General, United States Army Forces in South Korea, to Guard Colonel General I. M. Christiakov, Commanding General, Soviet Forces in North Korea, June 15, 1946:

"Although it has been more than one month since I wrote you suggesting we meet to discuss and clear up between us

American-Soviet Commission, Seoul, January 1946. *Lieutenant General John Hodge and Colonel General T. F. Shtikov.*

any misunderstood points of difference between our two delegations on the US-Soviet Joint Commission, I have not had the honor of a reply.

"As indicated in my letter, the American Command stands ready to resume negotiations in the Joint Commission at any time you suggest, in order fully to carry out the Moscow decision in accordance with the principles of freedom of expression as enunciated in the Atlantic Charter to which both of our governments have adhered. . . ."

Letter from Colonel General Christiakov to Lieutenant General Hodges, August 6, 1946:

"... Regrettably, your letter did not state whether the American Delegation in the Joint Commission will uphold the exact fulfillment of the Moscow Decision and consult only with those parties and organizations and their representatives which fully, without reservations, support this decision and did not compromise themselves by active opposition to it."

Letter from Hodge to Christiakov, August 12, 1946:

"... There is nothing the U.S. Delegation can read into the Moscow Decision that requires or implies that only those parties and organizations are to be consulted by the Joint Commission which fully, without any reservations, support this decision and did not compromise themselves by active opposition to this decision. ... There is nothing in the Moscow Decision or in the general usage of the word 'democratic' throughout the world that restricts its application only to organizations or parties belonging to schools of social thought favoring certain classes in the community over others, which seemed to be the interpretation given in practice to the word by the Soviet Delegation. The American Delegation can apply the word 'democratic' only as it is applied in common usage throughout the world, which normally would exclude only parties or organizations opposed to popular rule by elected representatives and to equal rights for all classes of people."

Letter from Christiakov to Hodge, October 26, 1946:

"... the Soviet Delegation, being guided by the aims and spirit of the Moscow Decision, deems that it would not be

... **August 2, 1946.** Soviets begin recruiting and training a heavily armed North Korean army. ....

right to consult on the question of methods of fulfilling the Moscow Decision with those parties and those, who for tactical considerations, although declaring their support of the decision, at the same time make such stipulations which convert their statement of support of the Moscow decision into an empty declaration."

George C. Marshall, the American Secretary of State at the time this exchange of differing views was taking place, summarized what the argument was all about on April 8, 1947:

"Unfortunately the work of the Joint Commission became stalemated after a short time through the failure to agree on the definition of the word 'democratic' as it pertained to the representatives of the parties and social organizations mentioned in the Moscow Agreement to be consulted by the Joint Commission in its task of assisting in the formation of a provisional government."

There were attempts to break the stalemate. At one point, the Soviets decided that there should be an elected Korean Provisional Assembly with countrywide authority. However, Moscow insisted on a catch. There was to be an equal number of representatives from both sides of the dividing line. In his New York talk, Dean Acheson reflected:

"That was an interesting proposal because, of the 30,000,000 people in Korea, 20,000,000 live south and 10,000,000 live north of the 38th parallel and therefore, it was suggested that there should be equal numbers . . . it was said to be equal. . . . equal representatives of what? Not of the people who lived north and south. . . ."

Clearly, there were fundamental differences between the Soviets and Americans over both the definition of the word "democracy" and the basic notion of political equality. There were also differences about the idea of individual rights. A month after Secretary of State Acheson reflected on the beginning of the war, a Korean who knew much about both the North and the South, a former schoolteacher, Lee Jung Hok, talked to two Americans:

> "During the Japanese regime, I had finished Myong-shin High School in Chae-ryong. After I finished the high school, I went to my native town which was in Kyo-jong-myon in Ongjin-gun. My native town is located just north of the 38th parallel. I was a school teacher at a primary school. . . . [In late 1945] I crossed the 38th parallel into South Korea and enrolled in a special course at Tong-guk University in Seoul. I had not stayed in the university very long because of financial problems. Then I went back to my home in North Korea. When I returned to my home town, I was put in jail by the North Korean police for interrogation which was, by regulation, required for anybody who came from South Korea. I had been imprisoned for a week when I was released from the North Korean police station jail . . . I had 60 boys and girls I taught English and mathematics. . . . The social status of these school children was not so good from the Communist viewpoint because they were sons or daughters of the rich class. At least they were not under the category which the committee called 'good' social status. I, also, was not enjoying 'good' social status from the Communist viewpoint. Therefore, the Communists continually watched me. I was arrested by the North Korean police and was sent to the Haeju police station where I was imprisoned for a month. When I was released from the police station, I returned to the Institute and I taught for two months more. Then I crossed the 38th parallel for the second time down to South Korea."

Lee Jung Hok's case was not uncommon. Another involved a North Korean, Kim Yong Bok, who could not escape to South Korea. He described life in North Korea during 1947:

"There were many political and social organizations, some of which had been formed and some of which were being organized. All of them were fully communistic and I found no way to agree with them. Therefore, I kept quiet and tried to be inconspicuous. . . . During these days, many Communists interfered with my life because I did not join any particular organization and become an enthusiastic member. Therefore they had constantly kept their eyes upon me. Also, the village we were living in was a very poor village and my mother had quite a few acres of land, which put us in a category of rich landlords by comparison with the poor people in the village. The upshot was, they confiscated our land without payment, but I was not chased out of the village as the really rich landlords were. Also, from time to time, I was taken to their organizations for questioning. Thus, they had been bothering me in this way and that way, for the sole reason that I was not an enthusiastic member of their group.

"Until that time I had heard of communism, but I had never had any experience in a real Communist society. I first felt that I had lost my freedom, and I had no longer any intention of staying in the Communist society. While I was staying in the village that year, the Communists started to draft young people. Therefore, I had to hide myself in the mountains."

The North Korean draft law of 1947 was a clear signal to many Koreans that the Communists were going to build an army and conquer the South. There had been propaganda

. . . **November 14, 1947.** U.N. General Assembly approves a resolution advocating U.N.-supervised elections in Korea followed by the withdrawal of troops from Korea. . . . .

bombasts from the North's capital, Pyongyang, claiming the country would be unified by force. But drafting young northerners and building an army? That was not words—it was action. Some northerners who opposed the idea of war to unify the country took to the hills or escaped to South Korea. But there was another side. Dedicated Korean Communists, and there were many, were constantly indoctrinating their countrymen. Party cells and their followers became devoted to the goal of an egalitarian, Marxist society in a unified Korea. Some of the converts were sent by the Communist regime to clandestinely recruit party members or begin guerrilla warfare in South Korea. Others stayed in the North and contributed to the growth and strength of the North Korean Army. It would not be until months after the war had broken out that Americans would discover the fervor some northerners attached to the goal of Communist North Korea. The enthusiasm was made evident during interviews with some North Korean prisoners in 1952. Even though the northerners were told they would only be identified with numbers so that their beliefs could not become associated with their names, and even though in captivity they might expect retaliation if they uttered pro-Communist statements, a large percentage earnestly clung to the party line:

PRISONER #440: South Korea is a capitalist country where the people have no sympathy for one another. The rich lead good lives but the poor will never be better off.

PRISONER #645: America provoked war in order to colonize small countries and control the whole world. She sells her goods and enslaves many people. . . .

PRISONER #605: Russia liberated weak and small nations and helped them toward self-government. For the North Korean government, she provides instructors in military tactics, and

. . . **April 8, 1948.** President Truman directs withdrawal of U.S. troops from Korea. . . . **May 10, 1948.** South Korea holds U.N.-supervised election while Soviets bar U.N. from North.

The president and the general. *South Korea's President Syngman Rhee greets General of the Army Douglas MacArthur during the general's visit to Seoul, August 1948.*

    supplies arms, and politically, she is helping to put a democratic plan into effect. This is true assistance. Russia has no territorial ambitions.

PRISONER #646: The South Korean government is made up of monopolistic capitalists, so the will of the people is entirely ignored.

PRISONER #439: They [the Communists] called the government "Syngman Rhee's puppet government." They said Rhee was selling Korea to the U.S.

    This last prisoner, #439, had hedged his bet, preferring to express what he had been told, not what he believed. He spoke of Syngman Rhee, South Korea's elected President who had come to power in a democratic process begun in 1948. That election was observed and declared just by the representatives from nine nations, members of the United Nations Commission on Korea. The U.N. had attempted to resolve the U.S.-Soviet impasse by a countrywide election, but the Soviets refused to permit the Commission entry to the North. Elections were held in the North, but only those chosen by the Communists and approved by the Soviets appeared on the ballot. The U.N. Commission on Korea described the government of North Korea in 1949:

> "The Northern regime is the creature of the military occu-
> pant [the Soviet Union] and rules by right of a mere transfer
> of power from that Government. It has never been willing
> to give its subjects an unfettered opportunity, under the
> scrutiny of an impartial international agency, to pass upon
> its claim to rule. The claims to be a people's democracy and
> expressions of concern for the general welfare are falsified
> by this unwillingness to account for the exercise of power
> to those against whom it is employed."

In part, the hostility of the nine-nation U.N. Commission on Korea toward the North Korean government was due to that regime's growing threats and war posturing. Radio Pyongyang kept up a steady drumbeat of intimidating statements directed at South Korea. A typical example of these broadcasts was aired on September 7, 1948:

> "Today, our 30 million Koreans have created the sound,
> powerful, sole supreme organ of our sovereignty, the Su-
> preme Korean People's Assembly, which represents our

... **September 19, 1948.** Soviets inform U.S. that all their troops will be out of Korea by end of year suggesting U.S. do likewise. . . . .

true will, protects our interests and rights, insures a bound-less development of the fatherland as well as the everlasting happiness and freedom for succeeding generations. It does not tolerate any imperialist aggression, and will bring about unification for our fatherland, driving out American imperialists from South Korea without fail and smashing the South Korean separate puppet government fabricated by traitors in collaboration with American imperialists."

While the regime of Kim Il Sung, North Korea's Soviet-picked and -trained Communist leader, was undoubtedly a dictatorship, Syngman Rhee's government was hardly a model for the observance of human rights. But the government of the Republic of South Korea was freely elected by the people of the South. Not long after both Soviet and American combat units withdrew from North and South Korea respectively, in December 1948 and June 1949, the Peninsula became immersed in a sea of guerrilla bands, spies, political intrigue, suspicion, and growing armaments. Increasingly, there were armed clashes along the 38th parallel. Despite the fact that Kim Il Sung's northern government dominated a population only half that of Syngman Rhee's southern regime, the northern militarists had a head start. With a strong assist from the Russians, the Communists built their army much faster and stronger than the southerners. The North enjoyed some other advantages, as well. Secretary of State Acheson, during his 1952 New York talk, said:

"Although, as I have pointed out, two-thirds of the people lived in South Korea and only one-third in North Korea, the resources of the country were very inequitably divided. North of the parallel were the major industrial

---

. . . **March 21, 1949.** U.S. Embassy established in South Korea, American military relieved of responsibilities . . . .

facilities—the iron industry and the steel industry of Korea. There was also the chemical industry, which produced the fertilizers very largely used in the agricultural South. All these facilities were situated in the North. Almost every hydro-electric project was situated in the North. Furthermore, the North, by the policy which it was conducting, sent 2,000,000 refugees into the already crowded South and, by thus thinning out its population, was able to be self-sustaining in food whereas the South was not. Finally, all the basic minerals were in the North, so that it was impossible for the South to begin industries to take the place of those to which they were denied access in the North."

The North was not only better off industrially and agriculturally, it unquestionably had the better, more modern military force. Curiously, the Americans in South Korea were not aware of just how much better the northern armed force was. This fact only came to light a few months after the war had begun. In the midst of battle, the U.S. Army assigned Lieutenant Colonel Roy E. Appleman the task of finding out what had happened. Interviewing North Korean prisoners, studying reams of intelligence reports, and questioning the American military advisers who were with the South Korean Army prior to the start of the war, Appleman reconstructed the comparative military strength of both North and South Korea on the eve of hostilities:

"The North Korean Army in June 1950 was clearly superior to the South Korean Army in several respects: the North Koreans had 150 excellent medium tanks mounting

85-mm [millimeter] guns, the South Koreans had no tanks. The North Koreans had three types of artillery—the 122-mm howitzer, the 76-mm self-propelled gun, and the 76-mm divisional gun with a maximum range of more than 14,000 yards which greatly outranged the 105-mm howitzer of the ROK [Republic of Korea] Army with its maximum range of about 8,200 yards. In number of divisional artillery pieces, the North Koreans exceeded the South Koreans on an average of three-to-one. The North Koreans had a small tactical air force, the South Koreans had none. In the North Korean assault formations there were 89,000 combat troops as against approximately 65,000 in the South Korean divisions. Also, North Korea had an additional 18,600 trained troops in its Border Constabulary and 23,000 partially trained troops in three reserve divisions. In comparison, South Korea had about 45,000 national police, but they were not trained or armed for tactical use. The small coast guard or navy of each side just about canceled each other and were relatively unimportant.

"The superiority of the North Korean Army over the South Korean in these several aspects was not generally recognized, however, by United States military authorities before the invasion. In fact, there was the general feeling, apparently shared by Brigadier General William L. Roberts, Chief of KMAG (Korean Military Advisory Group), on the eve of invasion that if attacked from North Korea, the ROK Army would have no trouble in repelling the invaders."

How had the Americans been deceived? A year before the war began, U.S. military intelligence officers were withdrawn along with the American combat troops. The newly formed Central Intelligence Agency (CIA) was in charge of U.S. intelligence in Korea. In fact, the CIA had been operating in Korea

Understanding the mysteries of a jeep. *U.S. Army Master Sergeant Floyd Wilkerson of the Korean Military Advisory Group teaches South Korean soldiers how to maintain a one-quarter-ton American utility vehicle.*

for some time, evidently without the knowledge of American military authorities. Years later, in 1988, John K. Singlaub, the CIA station chief in Manchuria during the late 1940s, revealed how the Agency used Korean refugees in Manchuria to enter North Korea along the Korean-Manchurian border, traverse North Korea, cross the 38th parallel, and report in to a CIA officer who, unknown to the U.S. military, was operating in Seoul.

"When I was running espionage out in Manchuria into North Korea . . . I could make no [overt] arrangements for a safe house in Seoul. . . . [Singlaub then described how he dispatched one of his assistants to the South Korean capital under the noses of the U.S. military authorities in an "unofficial" capacity to retrieve and debrief the agents that had begun their journey from Manchuria. But the CIA officer also said these operations were not always successful.] If an agent who had come through the North arrived in South Korea, South Korean Police would often pick them up and I would never see them again."

Singlaub blamed U.S. military officers in the Far East for what would be labeled one of the century's great American intelligence blunders, but his accusation does not ring true. With the departure of U.S. combat forces in mid-1949, CIA operations were largely unfettered throughout the Korean Peninsula. However, as General Roberts' ignorance makes clear, the quality of U.S. intelligence did not improve. In large part, the reason Roberts and other American officials in Seoul were blindly confident was that they did not realize the large size of the North Korean Army. During the period of U.S. Army occupation, MacArthur's command had constantly battled with the CIA over the issue of Communist strength. CIA officer Jay Vanderpool recalls an incident in 1949:

"The problem was that President Truman was not satisfied with the conflicts of estimates of the North Korean military forces. The British and Chinese [Nationalists] were pretty well agreed that there were about 35,000 or 36,000 trained troops in North Korea. General Headquarters under MacArthur's G-2, General Willoughby, estimated there were about 136,000. . . . The President apparently was irritated and he said, 'What's the damn story. Send someone over there to find out and let me know the facts!'

So I was sent there to find out and let him know. I was out there about two months before I was pretty sure. . . . My estimate was about 36,000. MacArthur's staff estimate was in error."

MacArthur's estimate, of course, was far closer to the truth than CIA's grossly undercounted number. Although it may have had the numbers of North Korean soldiers wrong, the U.S. Central Intelligence Agency did give warnings. And yet, therein lay another intelligence problem. The official who had more to do with founding the CIA than any other, President Harry S. Truman, summed up this second failure best and then described how he was surprised:

"The intelligence reports from Korea in the spring of 1950 indicated that the North Koreans were steadily continuing their build-up of forces and that they were continuing to send guerrilla groups into South Korea. There were continuing incidents along the 38th parallel, where armed units faced each other. Throughout the spring, the Central Intelligence reports said that the North Koreans might at any time decide to change from isolated raids to a full-scale attack. The North Koreans were capable of such an attack at any time, according to the intelligence, but there was no information to give any clue to whether an attack was certain or when it was likely to come. But this did not apply alone to Korea. These same reports also told me repeatedly that there were any number of other spots in the world where the Russians 'possessed the capability to attack.'

"On Saturday, June 24, 1950, I was in Independence, Missouri, to spend the weekend with my family and to attend to some personal family business. It was a little after ten in the evening and we were sitting in the library of our home on North Delaware Street when the phone rang. It was the Secretary of State [Acheson] calling from his home in Maryland."

The war had started. For the next three years, one of the most oft-repeated statements about the Korean War was, "It's the wrong place, the wrong time, and the wrong war." This statement was originally uttered by an officer who was referring to a wholly different situation. But it seemed to say what many Americans believed. Wrong place? Two years before the bloody struggle broke out, the U.S. Joint Chiefs of Staff, the country's senior military officers, said Korea was "of little strategic value." Wrong time? Focus on the Russians, constant reports of danger in other spots, and lack of specific information on the North Koreans ensured America would be more unprepared for this conflict than it had been just eight years before at Pearl Harbor. But wrong war? Probably not. Wars before and after this one were fought for much less. At the heart of this war was a profound disagreement between the two most powerful nations on earth, a disagreement over the meaning of a word . . . *democracy*. At its core, that is what the Korean War was all about.

CHAPTER

2

"SIR, WE GOT COMPANY"

June 25–August 31, 1950

BY THE TIME a surprised President Truman was informed of North Korea's aggression, a full-blown invasion of South Korea had been in progress for more than eight hours. In Korea, it was 4 A.M., a rainy Sunday morning, when the Communist artillery had opened up all along the 38th parallel. Appleman's reconstruction of that day's events was mainly gained from interviewing some of the five hundred American advisers to the ROK Army:

"Captain Joseph R. Darrigo was the only American officer on the 38th parallel the morning of 25 June. He occupied quarters in a house at the northeast edge of Kaesong ... Darrigo awoke to the sound of artillery fire and soon distinguished shell fragments and small arms fire hitting his house. He jumped from bed, pulled on a pair of trousers, and, with shoes and shirt in hand, ran to the stairs where he was met by his Korean houseboy running up to awaken him. The two ran out of the house and jumped into Darrigo's jeep and drove south into Kaesong. . . .

"At the circle in the center of Kaesong, small arms fire fell near Darrigo's jeep. Looking off to the west, Darrigo saw a startling sight—a half mile away; at the railroad station which was in plain view, North Korean soldiers were unloading from a train of perhaps fifteen cars. Some of these soldiers were already advancing toward the center of town, and it was their sporadic fire which had struck near Darrigo. Darrigo estimated there were two or three battalions, perhaps a regiment, of enemy troops on the train. . . .

"The North Koreans timed their main attack against the Uijongbu Corridor, an ancient invasion route leading straight south to Seoul, to coincide with the general attacks elsewhere. . . . The main attack developed along two roads which converged at Uijongbu and from there led into Seoul. . . . The strong armored columns made steady gains on both roads, and people in Uijongbu, twenty miles north of Seoul, could hear the artillery fire of the two converging columns before the day ended. . . . At mid-morning, reports came in to Seoul that Kimpo Airfield [serving the South Korean capital] was under enemy air attack. A short time later, two enemy Russian-built YAK [a World War II vintage propeller-driven aircraft] fighter planes appeared over Seoul and strafed the main street. In the afternoon, enemy planes again appeared over Seoul. . . .

"The next major point of attack eastward across the peninsula was at Chunchon which, like Kaesong, lay almost on the Parallel. Chunchon was an important road center . . . and gateway to the best communication and transport net leading south through the mountains in the central part of Korea. . . . The plan was for the 2nd [North Korean] Division to capture Chunchon by the afternoon of the first day; the 7th [North Korean] Division was to drive directly for Hongchon, some miles below the Parallel.

"The 7th Regiment of the ROK 6th Division guarded Chunchon, a beautiful town spread out below Peacock Mountain atop of which stood a well-known and much admired Shinto shrine with red lacquered pillars. The two assault regiments of the North Korean 2nd Division moved to the attack early Sunday morning. . . . From the outset, the ROK artillery was very effective and the enemy . . . met fierce resistance. . . . The enemy made several local penetrations, but each time were driven back by counterattack. . . . The battle for Chunchon was going against the North Koreans. The failure of the 2nd North Korean Division to capture Chunchon the first day as ordered caused the North Korean II Corps to change the attack plans of the North Korean 7th Division [which was diverted] west to Chunchon. . . . Apparently, there were no enemy tanks in the Chunchon battle until the [North Korean] 7th Division arrived on the evening of the 26th. The battle lasted through the third day. The defending ROK 6th Division withdrew southward June 28 when the front had completely collapsed on both sides of it. The North Koreans entered Chunchon. Nine T-34 tanks apparently led the main body into the town on the morning of 28 June. . . .

"[Meanwhile, to the west] The ROK 1st Division held its positions for nearly three days and then, outflanked and threatened with being cut off by the enemy divisions in the

Uijongbu Corridor, it withdrew toward the Han River. On the northwest approach to Seoul, the 1st [ROK] Division fought a good and creditable battle.

"One anecdote of tragic consequences relating to General Paik [Sun Yup] and his ROK 1st Division might be mentioned here. On the 28th, American fighter planes under orders to attack any organized body of troops north of the Han River mistakenly strafed and rocketed the 1st Division, killing and wounding many soldiers. After the planes left, General Paik got some of his officers and men together and told them, 'You did not think the Americans would help us. Now you know better.' "

The U.S. Air Force and the U.S. Navy had been ordered into the fight by the Truman administration. Just how the decision was made was revealed by the Secretary of Defense, Louis A. Johnson, during U.S. Senate hearings a year later:

SENATOR RICHARD B. RUSSELL: Can you give us a resume of the development of events and decisions which led to the final decision to intervene militarily for the protection of South Korea?

JOHNSON: . . . The first knowledge I had of trouble in Korea was some time, an hour or two before midnight [Saturday, June 24, about the same time President Truman was being informed], when one of the wire services passed on to me what they had. . . . Many of us met the President at the airport on Sunday evening when he came in . . . (we) met again on Monday evening [June 26] and at that time the decision on motion of Secretary Acheson was made to send the Navy and the Air Force into that situation, the United Nations having met at 3 o'clock on the previous Sunday afternoon and declared North Korea an aggressor.

. . . **June 28, 1950.** Seoul falls to Communists . . . .

Action, decisive action, was needed. On Monday, June 26, Uijongbu had fallen to the tank-led North Korean 3rd and 4th Divisions. The same day, a South Korean firing squad executed a beautiful Korean girl on a hillside overlooking Seoul. The girl, reportedly a mistress of an American colonel, was charged with spying. Then, too, both the ROK government and Army headquarters began leaving the South Korean capital. The next morning, the U.S. Embassy and the American Korean Military Advisory Group (KMAG) headquarters left town. On the 28th, panic set in among those fleeing the rapidly advancing Communist forces. The Americans learned the ROK Army was going to destroy the bridges over the River Han, the broad, shallow waterway south of Seoul, despite the fact that ROK troops, Americans, and thousands of fleeing civilians might be trapped in the doomed city. Urged to delay the destruction of the bridges by a plea from the ROK 2nd Division commander, the ROK Army headquarters sent General Chang Kuk, the Army's operations officer, to stop the demolition. Appleman recounts:

". . . General Chang went outside, got into a jeep, and drove off toward the highway bridge, but he found the streets so congested with traffic, both wheeled and pedestrian, that he could make only slow progress. . . . He reached a point about 150 yards from the bridge when a great orange-colored burst of light in the night sky and a deafening roar announced the blowing of the highway bridge and the three railroad bridges. . . . The best informed American advisors in Seoul at the time estimate that 500–800 people were killed or drowned in the blowing of this [highway] bridge. . . .

"The premature blowing of the bridges was a military catastrophe for the ROK Army. The main part of the army, still north of the river, lost nearly all of its transport, most of its supplies, and many of its heavy weapons. Most of the troops that arrived south of the Han waded the river or crossed in small boats or rafts in disorganized groups. The disintegration of the ROK Army now set in with alarming speed.

"Seoul fell on the fourth day of the invasion [June 28]. At the end of June [Friday, June 30], after six days, everything north of the Han River had been lost. Remnants of four South Korean divisions were assembling on the south bank or still infiltrating across the river. . . .

"Of 98,000 men in the ROK Army on 25 June, the Army headquarters could account for only 22,000 at the end of the month south of the Han . . . days later . . . when more stragglers assembled south of the river, this figure increased to 54,000. But this left 34,000 completely gone in the first week of war—killed, captured, or missing."

Why hadn't the American pilots been able to stop the advance of the North Korean tanks? In addition to the airmen's inability to distinguish friend from foe as indicated by the above example, there was also the fact that the North Korean tankers grew more adept at avoiding U.S. aircraft as each day passed. This latter point was driven home months later when some of the northern tank crewmen who had become captives spoke about their experiences:

SECOND LIEUTENANT LEE IN JIN: In the early phases of the war, no attempt was made to conceal movement of tanks and they were deliberately exposed to view to lower (the) morale of the enemy. When air attacks began, night movements were resorted to.

SECOND LIEUTENANT WUN HONG KI: . . . [We] always moved at night but found that U.N. air would attack groves and

orchards even though tanks could not be seen, so profiting from the experience of others, (we) put tanks in buildings or destroyed villages where they could be easily camouflaged.
SENIOR CAPTAIN KWON JAE YOUL: . . . Sometimes, the route used was a secondary one . . . more free from air attack.

On Thursday, June 29, General Douglas MacArthur, the American military commander in the Far East, left his headquarters and flew to Korea. MacArthur had been placed in charge of the U.N. effort to assist the South Koreans and was directing the air and naval effort. Landing at an airstrip south of Communist-occupied Seoul, the general worked his way forward and conferred with Korean leaders and the American military advisers. He concluded that the South Koreans had no realistic plan or capabilities to stop the advancing North Koreans. He also recognized that U.S. air and naval action was inadequate. Returning to Tokyo, MacArthur sent a message to the Joint Chiefs of Staff in Washington—the message arrived Friday, June 30, at about 3 A.M.:

". . . The only assurance for the holding of the present line, and the ability to regain later the lost ground, is through the introduction of U.S. ground forces into the Korean battle area. To continue to utilize the forces of our Air and Navy without an effective ground element cannot be decisive.

"If authorized, it is my intention to immediately move a U.S. regimental combat team to the reinforcement of the vital area discussed and to provide for a possible build-up to a two division strength from the troops in Japan for an early counter-offensive."

President Truman, an early riser, was already dressed and shaven when he was called at about 5 A.M. Truman immediately

. . . **July 5, 1950.** American infantrymen in action against North Korean forces . . . .

approved the dispatch of the regimental combat team and promised an answer on the two divisions later. True to his word, dispatch of the divisions was permitted that same day. Mac-Arthur had four U.S. divisions in Japan, the 24th, 25th, and 7th Infantry Divisions and the 1st Cavalry Division, the latter organized and equipped just like the others. Additionally, there was a regimental combat team. All of these units were under-strength. Congress had recently reauthorized the draft. But, until the events of this Friday in June, there had been no pressing need for combat soldiers. There had been enough young Americans volunteering for the somewhat relaxed duties in the armed forces. Conscription had seldom been used. With Truman's action, all that changed. For now and for the next three years, there was an insatiable demand for foot soldiers to risk their lives in a faraway land in a new kind of armed conflict. During hurried deliberations with senators in the last week of June, the administration considered and discarded the idea of a declaration of war. Americans and the soldiers, sailors, and airmen from a number of other nations who were under MacArthur's command were told they were participating in a "police action."

The early efforts of American infantrymen in Korea were not encouraging. After an initial encounter, the U.S. soldiers fell back in the same way their South Korean allies had retreated. In truth, the Americans had little more than the ROK soldiers to stop the Communist tanks. The U.S. bazooka, an inadequate weapon even during World War II, did not have the power to penetrate the Russian-made T-34 tank. Months after the first disappointing encounters, the U.S. Army Chief of Military History, Major General Orlando Ward, directed Captain Russell A. Gugeler to discover what had happened. Gugeler was told to put the story in an easily readable form and to concentrate on combat actions from the foot soldier's point of view. Daily talking to or corresponding with battle veterans, using interview materials from

other historians, after-action reports, and prisoner interrogations, Gugeler reconstructed events. His first report
was mainly derived from two sergeants, Zack C. Williams
and Roy E. Collins, who, as infantry platoon sergeants,
were among those members of the 24th Infantry Division
who fought the advancing North Koreans in the early days of
July 1950:

" 'As soon as those North Koreans see an American
uniform over here,' soldiers boasted to one another,
'they'll run like hell.' American soldiers later lost this
cocky attitude when the North Koreans overran their first
defensive positions. Early overconfidence changed suddenly to surprise, then to dismay, and finally to the grim
realization that, of the two armies, the North Korean force
was superior in size, equipment, training, and fighting
ability.

". . . men of Company A [34th Infantry] at Pyongtaek
finished digging their defensive positions or sat quietly in
the cold rain. In spite of the fact that a column of enemy
tanks had overrun the Osan position and was then not
more than six miles from Pyongtaek, the infantrymen did
not know about it. They continued to exchange rumors and
speculations. One of the platoon leaders called his men
together later that afternoon [July 5] to put an end to the
growing anxiety over the possibility of combat. 'You've
been told repeatedly,' he explained, 'that this is a police
action, and that is exactly what it is going to be.' He
assured them that the rumors of a large enemy force in the
area were false, and that they would be back in Sasebo
[Japan] within a few weeks. . . .

"Sergeant Collins was eating a can of beans. He had

eaten about half of it when he heard the sound of engines running. Through the fog he saw the faint outline of several tanks that had stopped just beyond the bridge. . . . At the same time, through binoculars, Collins could see two columns of infantrymen moving beyond the tanks. . . . He yelled back to his platoon leader, 'Sir, we got company.' Lieutenant Robert Ridley, having been warned that part of the 21st [U.S.] Infantry might be withdrawing down this road, said it was probably part of that unit. 'Well,' said Collins, 'these people have tanks and I know the 21st hasn't any.' The battalion commander arrived at Captain [Leroy] Osburn's command post just in time to see the column of enemy infantrymen appear. Deciding it was made up of men from the 21st Infantry, the two commanders watched it for several minutes before realizing it was too large to be friendly troops. They could see a battalion-size group already, and others were still coming in a column of fours. At once, the battalion commander called for mortar fire. When the first round landed, the enemy spread out across the rice paddies on both sides of the road but continued to advance. By this time Collins could count thirteen tanks. . . .

"Within a few minutes the men from the enemy's lead tank returned to their vehicle, got in, closed the turret, and then swung the tube until it pointed directly toward Company A.

" 'Get down!' Sergeant Collins yelled to his men. 'Here it comes!'

"The first shell exploded just above the row of foxholes, spattering dirt over the center platoon. The men slid into their holes. Collins and two other combat veterans of

---

. . . **July 10, 1950.** American tanks in action. U.S. 25th Infantry Division lead elements arrive in Korea. . . . .

World War II began shouting to their men to commence firing. Response was slow although the Americans could see the North Korean infantrymen advancing steadily, spreading out across the flat ground in front of the hill. In the same hole with Sergeant Collins were two riflemen. He poked them. 'Come on,' he said. 'You've got an M1. Get firing.'

"After watching the enemy attack for a few minutes, the battalion commander told Captain Osburn to withdraw Company A, and then left the hill, walking back toward his command post, which he planned to move south."

Captain Leroy Osburn managed to keep A Company together, but a number of other 24th Infantry Division companies disintegrated during July. The division's commander, Major General William Dean, was captured by the North Koreans after he had successfully led a fight against oncoming enemy armor, accompanying a team of his soldiers armed with a new 3.5-inch bazooka, a weapon that could penetrate the T-34s. By the end of August, what remained of the 24th Division joined the U.S. 25th and the 2nd Infantry and 1st Cavalry Divisions behind the Naktong River. Additionally, the 5th Regimental Combat Team, the 1st Marine Brigade, and some welcome U.S. medium tanks joined in the defense. The Americans faced west, and their allies from the 1st, 6th, 8th, 3rd, and Capitol Divisions of the ROK Army faced north. This line, the Pusan Perimeter, was under unremitting, fierce attacks by the North Koreans. But now there was hope. General MacArthur summed up the situation:

"Our final stabilization line will unquestionably be rectified and tactical improvement will involve planned with-

3.5-inch rocket launcher team. *Unfortunately, American troops did not have this weapon in the early days of the war. They had a smaller version that was ineffective against the Russian tanks. The 3.5-inch version was hurriedly produced and rushed to Korea.*

drawals as well as local advances. But the issue of battle is now fully joined and will proceed along lines of action in which we will not, repeat, not be without choice. Our hold upon the southern part of Korea represents a secure base. Our casualties, despite overwhelming odds, have been

... **July 20, 1950.** U.S. 24th Infantry Division troops withdraw from Taejon, their commander, Major General William F. Dean missing, later captured........................

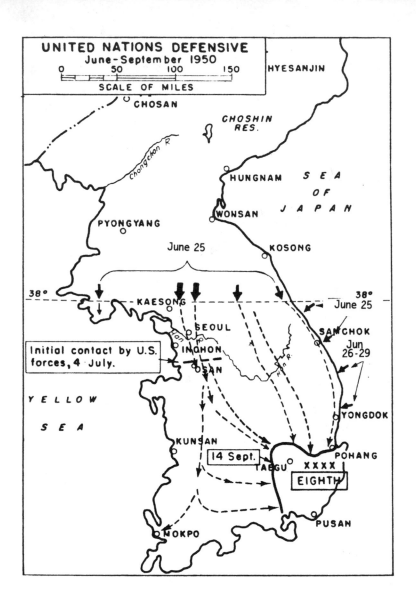

UNITED NATIONS DEFENSIVE
June–September 1950

SCALE OF MILES
0   50   100   150

HYESANJIN

CHOSAN

CHOSHIN RES.

Chongchon R

HUNGNAM

SEA OF JAPAN

WONSAN

PYONGYANG

June 25

KOSONG

38°   KAESONG   38°
                              June 25

SEOUL   SAMCHOK

Initial contact by U.S. forces, 4 July.   INCHON   Jun 26-29

SAN

YELLOW   YONGDOK

SEA

KUNSAN

14 Sept.   POHANG
        TAEGU   XXXX
                EIGHTH

MOKPO   PUSAN

relatively light. Our strength will continually increase while that of the enemy will relatively decrease. His supply line is insecure. He has had his great chance but failed to exploit it. . . .''

. . . **July 26, 1950.** U.N. forces withdraw into a loose defensive perimeter around the port of Pusan. . . . .

"HOME BY THANKSGIVING"

September–October 1950

THE WAR TOOK an abrupt turn in September. In the middle of the month, General MacArthur unleashed a dramatic and risky operation. It was the kind of heroic feat that had made him famous during World War II. The landing at Inchon cut off most of the North Korean Army then battling along the Pusan Perimeter more than 150 miles to the south. It gave the U.N. control of Korea's main north-south transport net and it opened the gateway to the ROK capital. The recapture of all South Korea assured, President Truman authorized the invasion and conquest of the aggressor state, North Korea. Before long, Pyongyang was in hand, and soon the Americans began hear-

September 1, 1950. Pusan Perimeter penetrated in an all-out North Korean offensive . . .

Pentagon luncheon, September 1, 1950. U.S. diplomatic and military officials confer. Secretary of Defense Louis Johnson seated to the far left. Secretary of State Dean Acheson is opposite Johnson to the right. The Joint Chiefs of Staff, several ambassadors, and the service secretaries are in the background. By the time of this meeting, the Joint Chiefs had sent their tentative approval of MacArthur's Inchon invasion plan to the Far East Command.

ing a tantalizing rumor: MacArthur wanted to wrap up this war quickly so the troops would be home by Thanksgiving.

The Inchon invasion had been planned by MacArthur's chief of staff, Major General Edward M. Almond. The operation featured an amphibious assault by U.S. Marines in a harbor

September 5, 1950. U.S. Joint Chiefs request MacArthur to reconsider his plan for an amphibious invasion at Inchon in view of threat to Pusan Perimeter . . . .

area whose tidal range of over twenty-nine feet only permitted landings during three hours in every twelve. Almond's scheme had the U.S. Army's badly understrength 7th Division following the marines to turn south and link up with northward-speeding forces breaking out of the Pusan Perimeter. Meanwhile the marines were to be seizing the city of Seoul. Since there were not enough available American soldiers to bring the 7th Division up to fighting strength, MacArthur, a few weeks before the landing, decided to flesh out the unit with hastily assembled South Koreans. A novel solution, this idea caused havoc for American supply officers. Lieutenant Colonel Charles R. Scherer and a quartermaster civilian official, Michael Slauta, recall:

SCHERER: We were preparing to go to Korea with a strength of about 9,000 when, about three weeks before our departure, we received 10,000 American and 8,000 Korean replacements to integrate into our division.

The Koreans we received looked as though they had been herded together to get them off the streets of Pusan. They spent their first week in Japan in quarantine, since they had to be deloused and cleaned. Then we had to equip them completely. . . . They could not speak English and we had few interpreters. Our instruction was given primarily by sign language and making simple motions for them to watch and imitate. . . . These men had no idea of sanitation, let alone the more complicated activities of military life.

SLAUTA: We had a considerable problem in issuing clothing and shoes to the South Koreans integrated into our ranks. They are very small people, standing only sixty-four or sixty-five inches, and are quite slender. Fortunately, they don't pay as much attention to size as we do. So long as an item was wearable, they would accept it and then trim it down.

. . . **September 8, 1950.** MacArthur informs JCS there is not the "slightest possibility" of U.N. forces being ousted from Pusan Perimeter . . . .

U.S. Marines landing at Inchon, September 15, 1950. *Many American military and naval officers doubted MacArthur and Almond's Inchon plan would work. It succeeded beyond all expectations.*

Footwear, however, was another problem. During the summer and fall of 1950, we were issuing all our footwear smaller than 6½ to ROK soldiers. There were some complaints of the fitting, so we ran a survey to see where we were going wrong. We found the mean size was 6 EE; the smallest ran down to 3½ EEEE; and the largest to 10½ EEE.

The landing at Inchon was near letter-perfect, but retaking

the ROK capital was another matter altogether. Along with a massive bombing effort by U.S. Air Force B-29s to destroy the transport system that the North Koreans would need to shift troops to the Seoul-Inchon region, five U.S. Navy carriers launched waves of planes to pound the defenders prior to the marines' assault. The first troops were ashore on September 15 and the all-important Kimpo Airfield was in marine hands on the 17th. The next day, the Army's 7th Division landed and began their linkup drive south. One of the Army's cameramen, Lieutenant Robert L. Strickland, however, was assigned to go with the marines and film the liberation of Seoul:

"We got across the Han River and caught an ambulance going up to the front. Almost from the time we left the river we were under sniper fire—not just occasional shots, but heavy fire. And most of the roads were under mortar fire, which made the going tough.

"When the ambulance turned off, I got off and started walking. We went a few yards and got pinned down with a group of marines by mortar and small-arms fire. I got a few shots of jeeps running under fire.

"From here we went up, one at a time, toward the real front. I hooked up with one outfit that was moving up and shot some scenes of them moving past a knocked-out North Korean tank. Then I got some shots of our tanks with flame throwers moving up with marines in the background.

"The next shot was a lulu. I am afraid that silent film can't do it justice. The tanks started moving through an opening in the sandbag barrier. There was one marine laying near the opening with his rifle pointed down the road. As the tanks moved through, all hell broke loose

. . . **September 11, 1950.** First U.S. Marine Division and 7th U.S. Infantry Division at sea, heading for Inchon. . . . .

from the enemy antitank guns and rifles. The marine by the opening jumped almost straight up and ran like a bat out of Hades. The spot he had been at had just got plastered, but I don't think he was hit.

"After that I shot some scenes over the sandbag barrier at the burning building in the background. It was exploding periodically. I didn't get a good explosion shot but I caught one section of the building falling with a terrific roar amid clouds of smoke and dust.

"I shot my next stuff at a road junction where some marines were running across the open toward a small, triangular building. There was a tank and a lot of buildings burning in the background. I finished shooting and ran across after them, stopping at the corner of the building to shoot again. About four men passed me from behind as I stood shooting up the street. All of them ran right into a mortar shell and got hit, one of them seriously. He got the one that was intended for me.

"I kept shooting while a couple of them picked up the seriously wounded man and helped him to hobble to cover. A few minutes later, an antitank shell came close enough to my left arm to ripple the sleeve of my jacket. I stepped back and looked around. By now there was a wounded marine and a wounded North Korean laying back of the burning building. Another marine with an automatic rifle was guarding them. I framed my picture so that they were in the bottom of the frame with the burning walls in the background. Then, right on cue, the wounded marine with his two buddies helping him along came hobbling into the frame for a great shot.

"Right after this we got so much fire of all kinds that I lost count. There were more mortar shells, more antitank stuff and more small-arms fire and then it started all over again. In a few minutes the little area back of the burning building which gave us cover was crowded with wounded men. They lay there in pain among burning debris and hot embers, hugging the ground to keep from getting hit again.

"There was only one medic—a Navy corpsman—so I put my camera aside and gave him a hand . . . I have seen a lot of men get hit both in this war and in World War II, but I think I have never seen so many get hit so fast in such a small area.

"I finally got free to start shooting again. . . . I started to get a low-angle shot of some marines coming across the road toward us. While I was getting down to shoot a mortar landed in the middle of them. I missed the burst but I got the camera going again as the smoke cleared. The guys in the street were running like mad. They headed for our little area, running all over me, but giving nice 'fade' by blocking the camera lens. I hung around long enough to get a shot of the litter bearers running for cover with one of the wounded men.

"For the next half hour or so, I couldn't seem to get back to shooting again. I guess I was a little shaky. The fighting had moved on up the road from me, and once you get out of it you find it awfully hard to get yourself back in it again.

"After fooling around for a while I worked down the road and stopped off in a kind of alley with a bunch of marines. I heard a tank coming up the road and I got ready to shoot. Just as the tank got into the frame, one of the marines fired a carbine about six inches from my nose. The camera lens went straight up and I was madder

. . . **September 26. 1950.** Seoul recaptured, U.N. forces from Pusan Perimeter heading north . . . .

than a wet hen—until I saw a sniper fall out of a tree behind me.''

Meanwhile, great advances were being made elsewhere. In one day, September 26, the 1st Cavalry Division smashed through Communist forces and raced one hundred miles northward, linking up with the 7th Division below Seoul. With the ROK capital in Allied hands, the marines moved north, reaching ten miles above the city by October 1. However, on the same day, the ROK Army, outstripping the progress of most American units, crossed the 38th parallel along the east coast of the Peninsula. By October 9 the 1st Cavalry Division crossed the parallel and moved into North Korea. All of this welcome news was reviewed in a meeting between General MacArthur and President Truman on Wake Island. After the session, Truman stated:

"I have met with General of the Army Douglas Mac-Arthur for the purpose of getting first-hand information and ideas from him. I did not wish to take him away from the scene of action in Korea any longer than necessary, and, therefore, I came to meet him at Wake. Our conference has been highly satisfactory. . . .

"I asked him for information on the military aspects. . . . I got from him a clear picture of the heroism and high capacity of the United Nations forces under his command. We also discussed the steps necessary to bring peace and security to the area as rapidly as possible in accordance with the intent of the resolution of the United Nations General Assembly and in order to get our armed forces out of Korea as soon as their United Nations mission is completed."

. . . **October 1, 1950.** South Korean units cross 38th Parallel heading north . . . .

U.S. infantrymen leading tanks out of the Pusan Perimeter. Once the breakout occurred, the North Korean Army was caught between the two arms of the U.N. forces. The Communists were soundly beaten and fled north.

Later, during congressional hearings, the analysis Mac-Arthur gave to the President at the Wake Island visit revealed what the general stated about the probability of Chinese intervention. MacArthur had observed:

"Had they interfered in the first or second months, it would have been decisive. Now we are no longer hat in hand. The Chinese have 300,000 men in Manchuria. Of

. . . **October 9, 1950.** President Truman and General MacArthur confer on Wake Island.

these probably not more than 100,000 to 125,000 are distributed along the Yalu River. Only 50,000 to 60,000 could be gotten across the Yalu River. They have no air force. Now that we have bases for our air force in Korea, if the Chinese tried to get down to Pyongyang, there would be a great slaughter. . . ."

As the U.N. Army moved north, some of the North Korean citizens, such as Kim Chang Song, who had opposed the Communists began to take revenge:

Mustangs wearing tiger teeth. *General MacArthur placed great reliance on American air superiority and air-delivered firepower. This photo, taken in October 1950, shows two World War II–vintage F-51 American fighters, on a South Korean landing strip.*

"I was listening every night and every day [to a radio] and was familiar with the United Nations forces frontlines. I heard United Nations forces had arrived at Nanchon. It was October 6, 1950. Knowing the U.N. forces had arrived at Nanchon, I started a movement from the mountains for my people.

"I put out an order to the high school boys in my home town to be ready to fight when the United Nations forces approached my town, and I also put out an order to the merchants in the market who were not watched very closely by the Communists, and told them to prepare themselves for fighting which would be taking place in the near future. . . . First of all, I had to gather some weapons to fight the enemy . . . I was lucky to get five North Korean Army [NKA] soldier uniforms and caps and I had those five uniforms put on my men so that they would be disguised. . . . We ambushed the NKA. . . . There was an NKA truck with some men . . . and we had our five men stop the truck and they were talking back and forth . . . then three of us hit and killed them.

"One of my men drove back. . . . We obtained 108 Russian rifles. We oiled those rifles overnight on October 12, 1950. I had all my people who were hiding in the ceilings of houses, in the fields and in the mountains gather at one place. . . . we attacked the enemy police station. We started opening fire at 9 o'clock [October 13]. . . . We found 80 anti-Communist youths in jail. We opened the door and we released them from the jail. There was a big air raid shelter in the back yard of the station and we found about 150 corpses of the friendly people who were killed by the Communists. . . . The corpses which we found made us cruel, our blood hot. Any Communists we found in town, we just killed them. . . . We lost about 100 friendly people in the fight. We killed every Communist we found and a great slaughter had taken place. The people in that area were embodied with the spirit of slaughter. . . .

"In that fighting we captured thirteen enemy trucks . . . a lot of heavy machine guns and rifles. We captured the chief committeeman of the province. We also captured twenty-three North Korean Army prisoners and one Russian woman. The Russian woman was the treasurer of a theater and was escaping in a car with the provincial committeeman. She had a baby with her that was very little at the time. I can't remember her name. . . .

"On October 19 U.N. forces arrived in my town without any fighting at all. It was the 187th [U.S. Army 187th Regimental Combat Team, a parachute unit commanded by Colonel William C. Westmoreland, who would later command U.S. troops in Vietnam.]. . . . When the first troops came in that area . . . there was a unit that looked pretty tough. . . . they took all the weapons from us. I went to the troops and explained what I had done in the town and I explained we were loyal people and I showed [them] the two prisoners. The troops took the woman with them and turned the chief back to us and we shot him. I asked for the weapons back and after a long talk I got about one third of the weapons back from them. . . . The UN forces kept going up north. . . ."

As the rapid advance continued, there was a gradual role reversal taking place. Just as the North Koreans experienced serious supply shortages in July when they were moving south, now, in late October, it was the Americans and South Koreans who could not seem to get what they needed. They were too far from their supply bases in the South. Quartermaster officer Major James W. Spellman of the U.S. 24th Division:

. . . **October 19, 1950.** U.S. Army captures North Korean capital, Pyongyang . . . .

Dealing with a North Korean machine gun. *A 57-mm recoilless rifle team knocks out a Communist machine-gun position, fall 1950. Left to right: Sergeant Ron J. Gladstone, Corporal John McCullough, and Private John L. Robinson.*

"Shoes are tied with scraps of cord and kitchens are using toilet soap received from home by mail. . . . It was understandable that supply confusion should exist at first, but I do not understand why the supply authorities should resist our legitimate requests telling us that we are using too much. . . . So long as Pusan remained within truck distance, it was possible to bypass approving authorities and go directly to the mountains of supplies in the port. Often

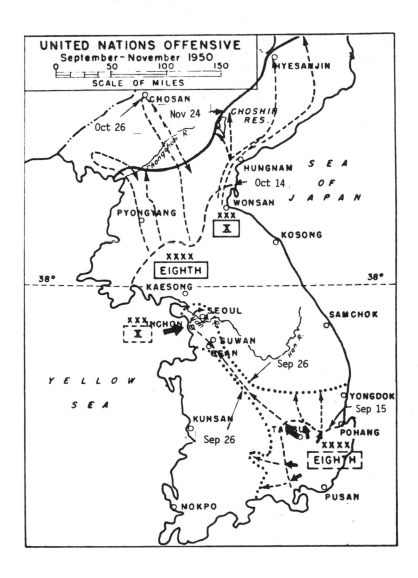

UNITED NATIONS OFFENSIVE
September–November 1950

0   50   100   150
SCALE OF MILES

CHOSAN
Nov 24
Oct 26
CHOSHIN RES.
HYESANJIN

Chongchon R.

HUNGNAM
Oct 14
WONSAN
SEA OF JAPAN

PYONGYANG

X
KOSONG

XXXX
EIGHTH

38°   38°

KAESONG

SEOUL
SAMCHOK

XXX
INCHON
X

SUWAN
OSAN
Sep 26
Han R.

YELLOW
SEA
YONGDOK
Sep 15

KUNSAN
Sep 26
TAEGU
POHANG

XXXX
EIGHTH

MOKPO
PUSAN

53

we obtained supplies in Pusan that were impossible to get through the red-tape maze of proper channels. Personnel in charge of the warehouse operations frequently begged us to take supplies so they could make room for those being unloaded from ships. . . . Even now, if a unit is willing to send its trucks 230 miles to Ascom City [near Seoul], or 400 miles to Pusan, supplies can be obtained. But the price in broken springs and deadlined [immovable] trucks is prohibitive.

"As the drive passed Kaesong, Pyongyang, and points north, frantically worded [supply] requests to Pusan awaited the opening of the shaky [Korean] rail system for delivery.

"In the prosecution of a war, the lack of a generator for a field range is not vital. But the result of poor meals is lowered morale—which is vital. When repeated supply failures occur, when indifference is shown, troops often become discouraged and indifferent. Supply failures at this level cost men their lives."

Supply difficulties, as serious as they were, paled in comparison to the rising alarm about the numbers of Chinese troops that were captured along the route north. At first, there was the notion that these new enemies might simply be individual replacements for the badly depleted ranks of the North Koreans. After all, there was need enough. The Allies had taken 135,000 North Korean prisoners since the Inchon invasion and breakout from the Pusan Perimeter. But, as the American representative to the United Nations, Warren Austin, pointed out to the Secretary General, there were growing indications of entire Chinese units. Most of this evidence was picked up from prisoners being taken by the ROK Army, the U.N. element that was farthermost to the front of MacArthur's troops.

"16 October: The 370th Regiment of the 124th Division of the Chinese Communist 42nd Army, consisting of approximately 2,500 troops, crossed the Yalu River at Wan Po Jin, and proceeded to the area of the Chosin and Fusen Dams in North Korea. . . .

"20 October: A Chinese Communist Task Force known as the 56th unit consisting of approximately 5,000 troops crossed the Yalu River at Antung and deployed to positions in Korea south of the Sui-Ho Dam. A captured Chinese Communist soldier of this Task Force states that his group was organized out of the regular Chinese Communist 40th Army stationed at Antung, Manchuria.

"30 October: Interrogation of nineteen Chinese prisoners of war identified two additional regiments of the 124th Division, the 371st and 372nd, in the vicinity of Changin."

A bone-chilling cold started settling in. Among the American troops, there was still talk of being home by Thanksgiving.

CHAPTER 4

DEFEAT OF THE U.N. ARMY

November 1–December 25, 1950

ALTHOUGH THE INITIAL indications of Chinese involvement did not seem seriously menacing at first, steadily mounting reports of Chinese infantry moving into Korea caused General Mac-Arthur to act. As indicated in his Wake Island response to President Truman's query about the possibility of Chinese intervention, the general resorted to airpower. Beginning on November 5, a massive air campaign was launched. Allied airmen went all out to stop the southward flow of Communist men and matériel. The failure of these efforts became painfully evident in late November. U.N. forces were soundly defeated and driven pell-mell all the way out of North Korea by the Chinese

November 2, 1950. Scattered Chinese Communist attacks on American units. . . . .

Army. For Americans, it was one of the most shameful and stunning military reversals in almost two centuries of armed conflict. The most shocking aspect of the collapse was the nature of the opponent. China fielded a rather primitive force, one with few airplanes and no navy to speak of. Chinese strength lay in its foot soldiers and a modest but well-handled artillery arm. Apparently, that was enough. Another remarkable aspect of this defeat was the brutal weather conditions. Many Chinese and some Americans froze to death in these two months. Some of the Americans died in this way through

And then the snow came. December 1950. A bivouac area of the 187th airborne infantry. In their haste to rush to the Yalu River, some American commanders failed to properly equip their soldiers for the bone-chilling cold reaching down from Manchuria.

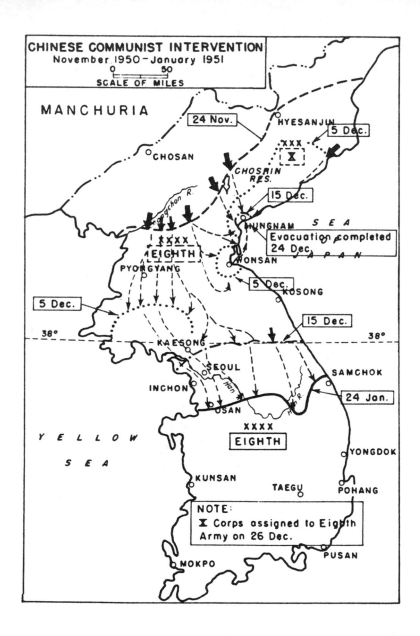

CHINESE COMMUNIST INTERVENTION
November 1950 – January 1951

0   50
SCALE OF MILES

MANCHURIA

24 Nov.

HYESANJIN

5 Dec.

XXX
X

CHOSAN

CHOSIN
RES.

15 Dec.

Kongchon R.

HUNGNAM   S E A

XXXX
EIGHTH

Evacuation completed
24 Dec.

PYONGYANG

WONSAN

J A P A N

5 Dec.

KOSONG

5 Dec.

38°   38°

KAESONG

15 Dec.

SEOUL

SAMCHOK

INCHON

Han

24 Jan.

OSAN

XXXX
EIGHTH

Y E L L O W

YONGDOK

S E A

KUNSAN

TAEGU

POHANG

NOTE:
X Corps assigned to Eighth
Army on 26 Dec.

MOKPO

PUSAN

negligence. A clearly frustrated William F. Pounder, a civilian who worked for the U.S. Army's Quartermaster General in Korea, spoke about this tragedy a month after it happened:

> "The primary reason for my trip to the Far East was to establish and execute a broad training program for all troops in Korea in the proper issue, fitting, use and maintenance of wet-cold and dry-cold climate clothing. . . . First, I feel that many staff officers are ignorant of proper clothing needs for cold-weather warfare. In October, at the time of our northern push, the troops left Seoul, Taegu, and Pusan—areas where the weather is comparable to that of Washington or Baltimore—and moved 150 or 200 miles north into areas with the climate of Maine—with only one layer of wool clothing. . . . I was told that, at this time, ammunition, POL [petroleum products], and rations had number one priority, and that when the cold weather came the supply of overcoats would be taken care of in due course. 'The supply of overcoats'! The supply of overcoats is not all that is concerned in cold-weather clothing."

The Chinese attack came at many different places and at varied times all along the front during November. Some U.N. units fared better than others, but all had to withdraw. Perhaps the most serious defeat of an American unit was experienced by the 1st Battalion of the 32nd Infantry. This sad story was told to a U.S. Army historian, Captain Martin Blumenson, not long after it happened. Blumenson's informants included a number of the survivors: the battalion's operations officer, Major Wesley J. Curtis, Lieutenant James G. Campbell, Sergeant John Doritsky, Private Royce Jensen, Private Gainius E. Woodhy, and Corporal Edward Deland. The battalion, along with many

. . . **November 21, 1950.** U.S. 17th Infantry reaches Yalu River . . . .

of its 7th Infantry Division sister units, was intertwined with the U.S. Marines in the northwestern part of North Korea. It was en route to the Chosin Reservoir. The story began on November 25, 1950:

"It was bitter cold . . . some of the men had listened to a news broadcast from Tokyo describing the beginning of a United Nations offensive in Korea designed to terminate the war quickly. Originating in General of the Army Douglas MacArthur's headquarters, the report predicted that U.S. divisions would be back in Japan by Christmas. It had been cheering news. . . .

"One regiment of the 7th Division—the 17th Infantry—had gone more than one hundred miles north of Hungnam and had reached the Yalu River on November 21. Other units of the division were separated by straight-line distances of more than seventy or eighty miles.

"At least one or two men from each company were frostbite casualties late that afternoon when the battalion closed into defensive positions [November 27]. . . . The night was quiet. There were warm-up tents behind the crests of the hills and the men spent alternate periods manning defensive positions and getting warm. . . .

"The marines had told Colonel Faith [Lieutenant Colonel Don C. Faith, the battalion commander] that several Chinese prisoners had revealed the presence of three fresh divisions operating in the area of the reservoir. Their mission, the prisoners said, was to sever the American supply route. The marines also told Faith's men that on the previous night, in this same location, a Chinese patrol had pulled a marine from his foxhole, disarmed him and beaten him.

. . . **November 26, 1950.** Chinese launch all-out attack shattering center of U.N. line . . . .

"The enemy attacked [on the night of November 27]. Probing patrols came first. . . . A few minutes after midnight, the patrolling gave way to determined attack. . . . The defensive perimeter began to blaze with fire. In addition to directing steady mortar and small arms fire against Colonel Faith's battalion, the Chinese kept maneuvering small groups around the perimeter to break the line. As one enemy group climbed a steep ridge toward a heavy machinegun operated by Corporal Robert Lee Armentrout, the corporal discovered he could not depress his gun enough to hit the enemy. He then picked up his weapon, tripod and all, cradled it in his arms and beat off the attack.

"After intense and confused fighting during the hours of darkness, the enemy withdrew at first light. . . . Sixty or more casualties gathered at the battalion aid station during the day. By evening, about twenty bodies had accumulated in front of the two-room farm house in which the aid station was operating.

"During the afternoon of November 28 a helicopter landed in a rice paddy near the battalion's command post buildings. General Almond [the corps commander, and perhaps one of the least admired of MacArthur's senior commanders], on one of his frequent inspections of his front lines, stepped out of the craft. He discussed the situation with Colonel Faith. Before leaving, General Almond explained that he had three silver star medals in his pocket, one of which was for Colonel Faith. He asked the colonel to select two men to receive the others, and a small group to witness the presentation. Colonel Faith looked around. Behind him, Lieutenant F. Smalley, Jr., a platoon leader who had been wounded

---

. . . **November 27, 1950.** Chinese attack Task Force Faith near Chosin Reservoir . . . .

the night before and was awaiting evacuation, sat on a water can.

" 'Smalley,' said Colonel Faith, 'come over here and stand at attention.'

"Smalley did so. Just then the mess sergeant from Headquarters company [Sgt. George A. Stanley] walked past. . . .

" 'Stanley,' the colonel called, 'come here and stand at attention next to Lieutenant Smalley.'

"Stanley obeyed. Colonel Faith then gathered a dozen or more walking wounded, drivers, and clerks—and lined them up behind Smalley and Stanley.

"After pinning the medals to their parkas and shaking hands with the three men, General Almond spoke briefly to the assembled group, saying in effect: 'The enemy who is delaying you for the moment is no more than remnants of Chinese divisions fleeing north. We're still attacking and we're going all the way to the Yalu. Don't let a bunch of Chinese laundrymen stop you.'

"Unfolding his map, General Almond walked over and spread it on the hood of a nearby jeep and talked briefly with Colonel Faith. . . . and then departed. As the helicopter rose from the ground, Colonel Faith ripped the medal from his parka with his gloved hand and threw it down in the snow. His operations officer [Major Wesley J. Curtis] walked back to his command post with him. 'What did the General say?' Curtis asked, referring to the conversation at the jeep.

" 'You heard him,' muttered Faith; 'remnants fleeing north!' [This unusual behavior might be attributed to the fact that during World War II, Don Faith had been the aide to General Matthew B. Ridgway, one of the U.S. Army's most respected combat leaders.]

"Just before dark, . . . November 28, planes struck what appeared to be a battalion-size enemy group that was marching toward the battalion perimeter. . . . [After this attack, being surrounded and with over one hundred wounded, Faith was ordered to] abandon as much equipment as necessary in order to have enough space on the trucks to haul out the wounded, and then attack south. . . . Movement of the 1st Battalion's column got under way just before dawn, November 29.

"Colonel Faith assembled as many men as he could and led them in a skirmish line directly across the ice. As it happened, a company-size enemy force was preparing to attack . . . when Faith's attack struck this force in the rear. Disorganized, the Chinese fell apart. Faith's men killed about sixty Chinese and dispersed the rest. . . .

"Rations were almost gone. Ammunition and gasoline supplies were low. The men were numbed by the cold. Even those few who had managed to retain their bedrolls did not dare fall asleep for fear of freezing. . . .

"Colonel Faith's task force beat off enemy probing attacks that harassed his force during the night of November 29–30. It was another cold morning. . . . Hopefully, the men decided they had withstood the worst part of the enemy attack. Surely, they thought, a relief column would reach the area that day. . . .

"During the night [November 30] Lieutenant Robert D. Wilson had directed mortar fire, but the ammunition was gone by this time. Assembling a force of twenty or twenty-five men, he waited a few minutes until there was enough light. His force was short of ammunition—completely out of rifle grenades and having only small arms ammunition and three hand grenades. Lieutenant Wilson carried a recaptured tommy gun. When daylight came the men moved out, Wilson out in front, leading. Near the objective an enemy bullet struck his arm, knocking him to the ground. He got up and went on. Another bullet struck him in the arm or chest.

" 'That one bit,' he said, continuing. A second or two

later, another bullet struck him in the forehead and killed him.

"Sergeant Fred Sugua took charge and was, in turn, killed within a few minutes. Eventually, the remaining men succeeded in driving the Chinese out of the perimeter. . . .

"Even after daylight, which usually ended the enemy attacks, the Chinese made one more attempt . . . Colonel Faith appeared at the aid station, asked all men who could possibly do so to come back on line.

" 'If we can hold out forty minutes more,' the colonel pleaded, 'we'll get air support.'

"There was not much response. Most of the men were seriously wounded.

" 'Come on, you lazy bastards,' Faith said, 'and give us a hand.'

"That roused several men including Lieutenant [James G.] Campbell. Because he could not walk, he crawled twenty yards along the railroad track and found a carbine with one round in it. Dragging the carbine, Campbell continued to crawl to the west. He collapsed into a foxhole before he reached the lines, and waited until someone helped him back to the aid station. This time he got in for treatment. The medical personnel had no more bandages. There was no more morphine. They cleansed his wounds with disinfectant, and he dozed there for several hours. . . .

"Task Force Faith had been under attack for eighty hours in sub-zero weather. . . . Few men believed they could hold out another night against determined attacks . . . Colonel Faith decided to try to break out. . . . He ordered the artillery and heavy mortar company to shoot up all the remaining ammunition before they destroyed their weapons. . . . [He] wanted the column to be as short as possible—only enough vehicles to haul out the wounded. . . . About noon, someone roused Lieutenant Campbell and said, 'We're going to make a break for it.'

"He and the other wounded men—several hundred of them by this time—were placed in the vehicles. They lay there for about an hour while final preparations for the breakout attempt were made. Enemy mortar shells began dropping in the vicinity.

"Colonel Faith selected Company C, 32nd Infantry, as advance guard for the column. Lieutenant Mortrude's platoon, the unit least hurt, was to take the point position for the company. Supported by a dual 40-mm half-track, this platoon would clear the road for the vehicle column. Mortrude, who was wounded in the knee, planned to ride the half-track.

"Friendly planes appeared overhead. Mortrude moved his platoon out about 1 P.M. Lieutenant Smith led out Company A. The men of these units had walked barely out of the area that had been their defensive perimeter when enemy bullets whistled past or dug into the ground behind them. At almost the same time, four friendly planes, in close support of the breakout action, missed the target and dropped napalm bombs on the lead elements. The half-track in which Mortrude planned to ride was set ablaze. Several men were burned to death immediately. About five others, their clothes afire, tried frantically to beat out the flames. Everyone scattered. Disorganization followed.

"Up to this point, units that had maintained organizational structure suddenly began to fall apart. Intermingling in panic, they disintegrated into leaderless groups of men. Most of the squad and platoon leaders and the commanders of the rifle companies were dead or wounded.

"Lieutenant Mortrude gathered ten men around him and proceeded to carry out his orders. Firing as they

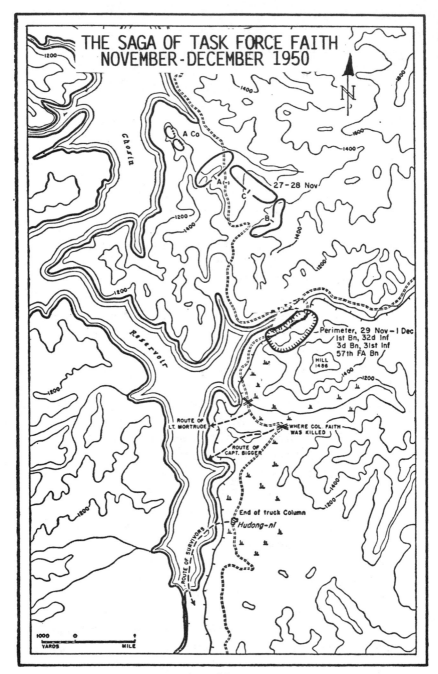

THE SAGA OF TASK FORCE FAITH
NOVEMBER-DECEMBER 1950

N

Chosin

A Co

A (—)

C

B

27-28 Nov

Reservoir

1200

1400

1200

1400

1400

1600

1400

Perimeter, 29 Nov–1 Dec
1st Bn, 32d Inf
3d Bn, 31st Inf
57th FA Bn

HILL
1486

1200

ROUTE OF
LT. MORTRUDE

WHERE COL. FAITH
WAS KILLED

ROUTE OF
CAPT. BIGGER

1400

1200

End of truck Column

Hudong-ni

ROUTE OF SURVIVORS

1200

1000   0

YARDS   MILE

advanced, they dispersed twenty or more enemy soldiers who fled. As they ran down the road screaming obscenities at the enemy, Mortrude and his men encountered several small Chinese groups, which they killed or scattered. . . .

"It was almost dark when Major [Robert E.] Jones [the battalion intelligence officer] and Colonel Faith, each with a hundred men or less, launched their attacks against the roadblock and knocked it out. Colonel Faith, hit by grenade fragments, was mortally wounded. A man next to him, hit by fragments of the same grenade, tried to help him down the road, but was unable to do so. Some other men came by, carried him down to the road and put him in the cab of a truck.

"Someone shouted for help to gather up all the men who had been wounded in the roadblock action. For half an hour the able-bodied men searched both sides of the road. When the column was ready to move again, the wounded were piled two deep in most of the trucks . . . Major Jones organized as many able-bodied and walking wounded men as he could—between a hundred and two hundred men—and started south down the road. . . .

"Private Glenn J. Finfrock (a machinegunner from Company D) became unconscious from loss of blood about the time the truck column came to its final halt. It was daylight on the morning of December 2 when he regained consciousness. He moved down the road a short distance until he found several wounded men trying to build a fire by one of the trucks—the one in which Colonel Faith had been placed the previous evening. His frozen body was still in the cab. Since the truck appeared to be in good order, Finfrock and another man tried unsuccessfully

. . . **December 2, 1950.** Lead elements of Task Force Faith reach friendly lines . . . .

to start it. As they were working on the truck some Chinese walked toward them from the village, and several men ran toward the ice. Others were captured. The Chinese gave morphine to several men, bandaged their wounds and, after caring for them for several days, freed them.

"Lieutenant Mortrude, wounded in the knee and in the head, walked to Hagaru-ri [a Marine Corps-held position with an airstrip]. It was 3:30 A.M., December 2, when he reached friendly lines. . . .

"On December 4, when most of its survivors had returned, the 1st Battalion, 32nd Infantry, counted only 181 officers, men and attached ROK troops, of the original 1,053 that had begun the operation."

Not all of the U.N. units had such difficulties in the withdrawal from North Korea, but a lot of American supplies, ammunition, and weapons were lost to the advancing Chinese and North Korean troops. However, some of MacArthur's units—for example, the 25th Infantry Division, which was on the western side of the Peninsula—largely pulled back in good order and lost little of its equipment. Lieutenant Colonel Barton O. Baker, the division's ordnance officer, recalls:

"Early in December the 25th Division was forced to withdraw by the Chinese offensive. Our SOP [standard operating procedure] provided the following order of march: division trains; service companies; two infantry regiments; ordnance armored maintenance platoon; tank battalion; the third infantry regiment; demolitions experts. The role of the ordnance armored maintenance platoon was to repair or evacuate any equipment that failed and, on call, to move back through the armor and last infantry regiment to service or evacuate equipment.

"When we reached the small village of Chunghwa we had twenty trucks we could evacuate no farther. These were placed near a crossroads and persons passing were invited to cannibalize them. A more serious problem, though, was the need to change eight tank engines. This had to be done before the platoon could proceed.

"The temperature was 10 degrees below zero that night. We pulled the eight tanks into an area near the crossroads of the town, erected tents, started bonfires, and went to work. We started at about 6 P.M. and by 6 A.M. all eight tanks had new engines and were on the road. It was a hard cold night, but Ordnance did its job. Before noon of that day the enemy was in Chunghwa."

By mid-December the full extent of the defeat of an American army in Korea at the hands of a Chinese army became known. With U.N. forces in full retreat, without an apparent ability for America's overwhelming air and naval superiority to make a difference, there seemed to be no hope for the United Nations to either repel the Chinese or even hold on in South Korea. Regardless of how bad it had been during the summer when the Americans and South Koreans had their backs to the wall on the Pusan Perimeter, this was worse. At least before, large numbers of U.S. troops and aircraft were on their way to Korea. Now all these forces and more were on hand but the Chinese kept coming. If some Americans were not fully aware of the prospects, they likely knew after the evening of December 15, 1950. By then, President Truman had spoken on a nationwide radio broadcast:

... **December 5, 1950.** Communist forces recapture Pyongyang ... **December 15, 1950.** President Truman tells Americans U.S. in "grave danger." ....

"I am talking to you tonight about what our country is up against and what we are going to do about it. Our homes, our Nation, all the things we believe in are in great danger. This danger has been created by the rulers of the Soviet Union.

"For five years we have been working for peace and justice among nations. We have helped to bring the free nations of the world together in a great movement to establish a lasting peace. Against this movement for peace, the rulers of the Soviet Union have been waging a relentless attack. They have tried to undermine or overwhelm the free nations, one by one. They have used threats, treachery and violence.

"In June, the forces of Communist imperialism broke out into open warfare in Korea. The United Nations moved to put down this act of aggression and by October had all but succeeded. Then, in November, the Communists threw their Chinese armies into the battle against the free nations.

"By this act they have shown that they are now willing to push the world to the brink of a general war to get what they want. This is the real meaning of the events that have taken place in Korea. That is why we are in such grave danger.

"The future of civilization depends on what we do—on what we do now, and in the months ahead. We have the strength and we have the courage to overcome the danger that threatens our country. We must act calmly, wisely, and resolutely. Here are the things we must do:

"First, we will continue to uphold and, if necessary, to defend with arms, the principles of the United Nations— the principles of freedom and justice.

. . . **December 23, 1950.** General Walker killed in jeep accident; Lieutenant General Matthew B. Ridgway announced as successor . . . .

"Second, we will continue to work with the other free nations to strengthen our combined defenses.

"Third, we will build up our own Army, Navy, and Air Force, and make more weapons for ourselves and our allies. . . ."

Whatever else the defeat of a United Nations army might have caused, it certainly provoked a massive mobilization in the United States, one that would last for almost forty years.

5

MATTHEW B. RIDGWAY AND THE RENAISSANCE

December 26, 1950–April 11, 1951

THE REVIVAL and resurgence of MacArthur's army in Korea took six weeks, about the same duration of its collapse in mid-November to late December 1950. The new year came with talk of civilization in peril still in the air, but before the first week in February 1951 was out, an entirely new atmosphere was brewing. The Allies stopped their flight from the North, turned around, held their ground, cautiously probed back toward the North, and then mounted a full-fledged and entirely successful offensive. There were any number of reasons for the renaissance, none more important than the courage, determination, skill, and actions of a single officer, Lieutenant General Matthew B. Ridgway.

Ridgway's battlefield appearance came when MacArthur's Eighth Army commander in Korea, General Walton Walker, was killed in a jeep accident near Seoul in late December 1950. U.N. forces were still reeling back, with no indication they would remain in Korea. There was talk the South Koreans might join the Communists and turn against the Allies. Arriving in Tokyo by plane from the United States on December 26, the former World War II paratrooper strode into General MacArthur's office and reported for instructions. Ridgway recalled the conversation:

"So when I talked with General MacArthur, I said 'If I find the situation to my liking, would it be agreeable to you if I go on the offensive?'

"MacArthur said, 'Matt, the Eighth Army is yours. Do what you like with it. You will make mistakes. I will support you.' "

Ridgway then flew to Korea, sending ahead a radio message to be read to all of the officers and as many of the men as possible. The brief passage announced the assumption of command and closed with the words:

"You will have my utmost. I shall expect yours."

Arriving at his headquarters, he found it was 180 miles to the rear of his forwardmost troops and promptly rejected staying

... **December 30, 1950.** First mass flight of Communist MiG-15 jet fighters attack U.S. jets near Yalu River . . . .

there, initially preferring to move in with one of the corps command posts, closer to the front. In later years, the general summarized his first few days in Korea:

"Within forty-eight hours or so, I had visited every corps and division commander. . . . When I would go up front to visit the battalions, I would say, 'Your infantry predecessors would roll over in their graves about the way you have been conducting operations here. You're road bound. You can't get off the road. You say you don't have communications. You've got runners. Use them! Get up in the hills and take the high ground.'

"They [the U.N. commanders] knew if I was up there, if I was up there myself, my principal purpose was to get the quickest and most accurate picture of the situation and to help them, not interfere in any way, but to help them. Particularly, I found this in the early stages, they weren't using more than a third of the firepower they had available to them. It was back in the column on the road somewhere, but unused. . . .

"I asked one man what his particular gripe was. He wanted to write home but he never got any stationery to write on. So, I had somebody send up a supply of stationery to that particular unit that night marked for this soldier. . . . I would take extra pairs of gloves along. . . . Any soldier up there—you know—the temperature is down below or around zero and his hands are cold and raw . . . the general gives his gloves to front line soldiers. . . . Word gets around about those things. . . ."

Sergeant Harry G. Summers, Jr., of the 24th Division remembers:

"We heard this story. Ridgway was moving up to the front in a jeep. Some outfit was retreating and one of the overloaded machinegunners was plodding along in the snow and slush, one bootlace untied. Ridgway hollers 'Stop!' The jeep skids to a halt. The general jumps out, trots back to the GI, stops him and kneels down in the mud in front of him. General Ridgway ties the man's bootlace, stands up and pats him on the shoulder. I never knew if the story was true or not, but it sure got around. I heard about five versions of it."

Lieutenant General Matthew B. Ridgway. One of America's best combat leaders. With X Corps officers, February 1951.

At first, Ridgway could not do what he wanted to do: attack. Much of his force was still at sea, being brought out of northeastern Korea to rejoin sister units that had come out of the northwest by road. His overall assessment was that "this army was in no condition for major offensive action." When the Chinese staged an all-out New Year's Day offensive, the Eighth Army commander knew he had to continue the retreat—giving up Seoul in the process. The most serious factor was that his South Korean allies could not be stopped in their flight. They were in a near panic in their move south. Ridgway:

"I had to pull back right away. I had these two understrength [U.S.] divisions north of the Han River. . . . [The ROK soldiers] had a very deep fear of the Chinese . . . even though some times you'd roll into your sleeping bag at night with a whole ROK division there, it would be gone by morning. They would pull out during the night and be ten to twenty kilometers to the rear by daylight."

Always in the thick of things, Ridgway attempted to personally stop an ROK division fleeing south from Seoul during the New Year's Day attack. Failing, he had to carefully plan the withdrawal, making sure the disaster of June 1950, when much of the South Korean Army was lost north of the Han River in panicked flight, was not repeated. He recalled standing in the path of a frantic ROK Army division bolting out of Seoul, waving his arms:

"I couldn't stop them on the road. The trucks came barreling down the road. They didn't try to run me down and some stopped. But I couldn't do anything with them. They had thrown away their weapons and everything. Not only

. . . **January 4, 1951.** Communist forces recapture Seoul . . . **January 8, 1951.** U.S. command learns of North Korean refugees on off-shore islands willing to fight Communists.

the crew served weapons, but everything. They just had their hands. Well, it was up to the U.S. 24th and 25th Divisions to do their best while we got it [the ROK division] in reasonable shape. . . .

"I gave them [U.S. leaders] instructions . . . personally, up there talking to the two corps commanders and all of their division commanders . . . there would be an orderly withdrawal. Then I had the 1st Cavalry Division south of the Han to cover the right flank, but they were so far understrength. I had very little confidence in the right half—east half—of the Peninsula which was wide open except for the Capitol Division of the ROK Army which was way over on the Sea of Japan coast. So, had the Chinese really increased their manpower and taken their casualties as they did later, they could have made it very rough for us there. If they had pushed a heavy force down at night—they were definitely adept at moving at night— around our right flank, which was well within their capabilities—we could have had a rough time. . . . Of course, then I was concerned that we only had one floating bridge across the Han, which was about the width of the Potomac in Washington.

"The Han River was tidal with lots of large cakes of ice. . . . There were over a million people in Seoul. And they just might flood that bridge and make it very difficult to control. That's why I pulled Charlie Palmer [Brigadier General Charles D. Palmer], the Assistant Division Commander of the 1st Cavalry Division, out and put him in charge of the crossing site . . . I had already notified the civilian government that we would start evacuating [Seoul] . . . they were to notify the civilian populace that under no circumstances would there be civilian traffic allowed on it [the Han bridge], or to cross it. I told Charlie Palmer he had my full authority to instruct his MPs [military police] there to use everything they could in the way of persuasion to keep civilians off the road if they tried to use it, but in the final analysis, if they couldn't, then they were authorized to fire on these people . . . I stayed there with him for the first few hours until after dark. . . . We never had the slightest incident. No interference from civilian traffic whatever."

Once again, the capital of South Korea was in enemy hands. Once again, the long lines of old men, women, and children carrying their pathetic belongings on their backs began streaming south following the retreating U.N. Army. This time the exodus was in the depths of a brutal, freezing winter. It all looked hopeless. With General Ridgway trying to rally his forces, President Truman attempted to impress on an increasingly restless and frustrated American public the importance of this distant war. On January 8, 1951, in his State of the Union address, the President said:

"Korea has tremendous significance for the world. It means that free nations, acting through the United Nations, are fighting together against aggression. We understand the importance of this best if we look back into history. If the democracies had stood up against the [Japanese] invasion of Manchuria in 1931, or the attack on Ethiopia in 1935, or the seizure of Austria in 1938, if they had stood together against aggression on those occasions as the United Nations has done, the whole history of our time would have been different."

In Korea Ridgway appeared outwardly confident and optimistic, but Brigadier General Walter F. Winton, the general's wartime aide, perhaps knew of the general's actual feelings:

"The Eighth Army . . . had been beaten up, punched around, disorganized . . . morale was nearly non-existent, and its rations were bad. The ROK's were in an even more miserable condition. The Chinese had them spooked. They were folding up and abandoning equipment worth millions of dollars with every Chinese attack. If you had been a betting man, you would not have bet an awful lot on the U.N. forces at this juncture in history. A short summation of the situation: weather, terrible; Chinese, ferocious; and morale, stinko."

The problem with the ROK forces was a vital consideration. The South Koreans composed about half the U.N. forces. They had always been behind their northern cousins militarily. North Korea had organized its army first. The northerners had been armed better than the southerners. Prewar North Korea had trained its leaders in regular, organized offensive combat by large formations, whereas the southerners had initially concentrated on constabulary or police-type actions. The costly, disorganized flight of the surprised, outmanned, outgunned ROK Army in the summer of 1950 had robbed it of some key leaders and what little confidence the fledgling force had attained in its short history. When President Truman sent one of his friends, a U.S. Army Reserve major general, Frank E. Lowe, to Korea, he received a firsthand report from his friend written during the dark days of early January 1951. Lowe wrote about what he considered to be the single most important consideration about the war: faulty leadership in the ROK Army. The general had a proposed solution:

"The point is that our [U.S.] lines are so thinly held and our forces so small that we must have support from the ROK forces and this requires leadership, at least from battalion upwards, that their officers are uniformly unable to give. Hence, my plea for our officers to have command authority, including disciplinary action over these units."

Lowe's analysis of the problem was undoubtedly flawless, but his solution was a bit impractical. First, the U.S., itself rapidly expanding its own forces for both Korea and Europe, did not possess an abundance of trained leadership. Second, the senior U.S. ground force commander in Korea, the commanding general of the Eighth Army, had been given command of ROK forces, so that, at least at the top, there was American leadership. But, at the lower levels, effective American leadership would require language-trained U.S. officers, leadership skills tailored to the Korean culture, and time to gain the confidence of South Korea's peasant soldiers. Then, too, at some point the ROK Army would have to develop its own leaders. The best the U.S. could do in these bleak cold days would be to put up enough of a fight to give the South Koreans the time to organize their own forces, train their troops, and nurture their future leaders. At this point, everything depended on the Americans.

Finally, retrieving some of the American units that had come south by sea, Ridgway organized a thinly manned defense line far south of the Chinese and began to plan a general U.N. offensive. The first task was to find out who, what, and where he would attack. He needed detailed intelligence, enemy dispositions, weapons, weaknesses, characteristics of their commanders, etc. Just at that time, the director of the Central Intelligence Agency arrived for a visit in Korea. Ridgway recalled:

> "Bedell Smith was head of CIA at that time. A friend of mine for years and Fort Leavenworth classmate. . . . I said, 'Bedell, this is deplorable. The whole intelligence effort of our government can only provide me with a goose egg out in front showing 174,000 Chinese.' . . . I told Bedell, 'The only thing I can do is go find out myself.'

. . . **January 15, 1951.** Communist offensive stalled, U.N. begins limited attacks . . . **February 1, 1951.** U.N. General Assembly, after a month of debate, brands China an aggressor.

"Then I got Pat Partridge [U.S. Air Force General Earl E. Partridge], who commanded the Fifth Air Force, and said, 'Pat, I want to go and have a look see for myself before I turn loose any major unit in an offensive action.' So, he piloted me himself and we went twenty miles deep into enemy territory at rather low level . . . we didn't see the enemy. . . . no smoke, no tracks in the snow. . . . That's when I said, 'Start by sending in one reinforced RCT [regimental combat team] with armor, in the day light. Let them go in a probe in there and be prepared to pull back to the line by dark and button up.' . . .

"By January 15, I was attacking with one division at a time from each corps. And shortly after, three weeks after, we got the whole Eighth Army moved forward in an offensive."

The first step on the way back was taken gingerly. It was just to gain contact with the enemy. That done, without a U.N. reversal, Ridgway determined the time was ripe for a serious slugfest. In mid-February an ugly fight broke out between an element of the U.S. 2nd Infantry Division, the 23rd Infantry Regiment, and growing numbers of Chinese infantrymen. There were elements of five Chinese divisions identified at the regiment's position, a spot called Chipyong-ni. The badly overmatched U.S. foot soldiers stubbornly held their ground despite mounting casualties. But the Communists were paying too. From the air, one could see the bodies of some 2,000 Chinese strewn around the encircled Americans. Recently arrived from the North, the corps commander, General Almond, requested to withdraw the U.S. regiment. Ridgway refused. The beleaguered regiment would not pull back, it would instead be reinforced. An armor-heavy infantry unit,

---

. . . **February 15, 1951.** U.S. establishes island support bases to aid North Korean partisans attacking Communist forces on the mainland . . . .

At the Han, one more time. *A U.S. tank crew overlooks the frozen Han River as an Air Force fighter-bomber drops a bomb on a Communist position on the northern bank.*

the 5th Cavalry, from the 1st Cavalry Division, located fifteen miles south was ordered north. Under the command of Colonel Marcel G. Crombez, a slimmed-down mobile task force was assembled and pushed out during the night of February 14. By dawn, it was halfway to Chipyong-ni, attacking against mounting Chinese resistance. Soon after the action, Captain Martin Blumenson interviewed the cavalrymen and recorded what happened:

". . . Colonel Crombez decided that only an armored task force would be able to penetrate the enemy held territory. . . . [He] separated the tanks—a total of twenty-three—from his regimental column and organized an armored task force. . . . He also ordered a company of infantrymen to accompany the tanks in order to protect them from fanatic enemy troops who might attempt to knock out the tanks at close range. . . . In addition, four combat engineer soldiers were ordered to go along to lift any antitank mines that might be discovered. The engineers and infantrymen were to ride on top of the tanks. . . .

"The task force, with fifty-yard intervals between tanks, proceeded about two miles—until the lead tank approached the village of Koksu-ri. All of the sudden, enemy mortar shells began exploding near the tanks, and enemy riflemen and machine gunners opened fire on the troopers exposed on the decks . . . the entire column came to a halt. The tankers turned their guns toward the Chinese who they could see clearly on nearby hills and opened fire with their machine guns and cannons . . . Colonel Crombez directed the tank fire.

" 'We're killing hundreds of them!' he shouted over the intertank communications.

"After a few minutes, however, feeling that the success of the task force depended upon the ability of the tanks to keep moving, Colonel Crombez directed them to continue. . . .

"During the next three or three and a half miles there were several brief halts and almost continuous enemy fire directed against the column. . . . Although enemy fire was causing many casualties among the troopers who remained on the tanks, Colonel Crombez, speaking in a calm and cool voice over the radio, each time directed the column to continue forward.

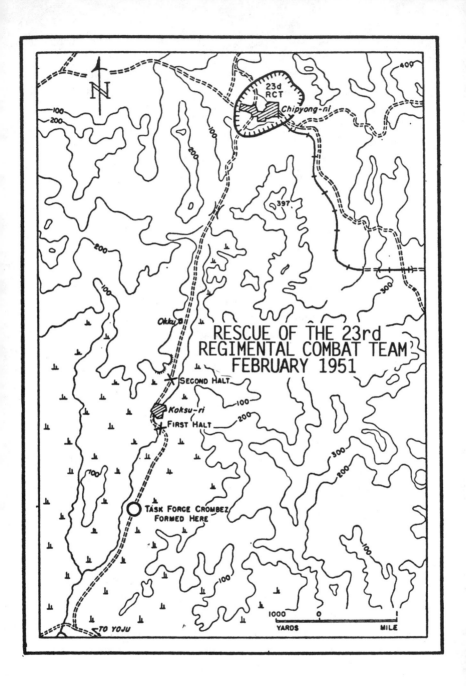

RESCUE OF THE 23rd
REGIMENTAL COMBAT TEAM
FEBRUARY 1951

23d RCT

Chipyong-ni

397

Okku

Second Halt

Koksu-ri

First Halt

Task Force Crombez
Formed Here

TO YOJU

1000   0

YARDS   MILE

"Meanwhile, within the perimeter of the 23rd RCT at Chipyong-ni, the 2nd Battalion was fighting off stubborn and persistent enemy attempts to overrun the sector shared by Company G, 23rd Infantry, and Battery A, 503rd Field Artillery Battalion, on the south rim of the perimeter. Late in the afternoon of 15 February, after twenty hours of uninterrupted fighting, the battalion commander managed to send four tanks a short distance down the road leading south beyond the regimental defense perimeter with the mission of getting behind the Chinese and firing into their exposed flank and rear. Ten or fifteen minutes of firing by the four tanks appeared to have suddenly disrupted the Chinese organization. Enemy soldiers began running. . . .

"By this time [when the linkup between the two U.S. forces was made] the Chinese were in the process of abandoning their positions south of Chipyong-ni and many were attempting to escape. Enemy opposition dwindled. With enemy soldiers moving in the open, targets were plentiful for a short time and Colonel Crombez halted his force long enough to take the Chinese under fire."

It had been costly and provoked some to question the worth of this war. Between the two units, the 23rd Infantry and Task Force Crombez, the casualties in dead and missing numbered into the hundreds. The bloody results of this fight and others like it stoked the debate that had been going on since mid-January when news of a U.N. peace initiative appeared in the newspapers. Secretary of State Dean Acheson tried to explain this turn of events:

"There has been a good deal of discussion in this country regarding the cease-fire proposal in the United Nations and why this Government voted for it. I should like to comment briefly on this matter. . . .

"The proposal was put forward by the Cease-Fire Committee—the President of the General Assembly, Mr. [Lester B.] Pearson of Canada, and Sir Benegal Rau of India. It had the support of the overwhelming majority of the U.N. members. This support was founded on two principal attitudes. One was the belief of many members that the Chinese Communists might still be prevailed upon to cease their defiance of the United Nations. While we did not share this belief, we recognized that it was sincerely held by many members.

"The second attitude was that, even though there might be little prospect in the approach to Peiping, the United Nations should leave no stone unturned in its efforts to find a peaceful solution. Holders of each view believed and stated to us that opposition or abstention by the United States would destroy any possibility of success which the proposal might have.

"If accepted, first, there would be a cease-fire in Korea. Then, after the fighting has stopped, there would be negotiations among all interested parties to find a peaceful settlement of the Korean question and other outstanding problems in the Far East. . . .

"We don't want our troops in Korea any longer than is absolutely necessary. . . ."

Even as Secretary Acheson was explaining the proposal, the Chinese were replying, demanding preconditions for talks on Korea: the withdrawal of U.S. forces from Taiwan and the replacement of Chiang Kai-shek's representatives at the U.N. with those of the Communist government on the mainland. Of course, the preconditions were rejected, but a dialogue of sorts had been opened. It was clear the Chinese wanted to talk, possibly because their troops seemed stalled south of Seoul. America's success or failure at this exchange largely hinged on the strength it could demonstrate on the battlefield: its ability to overcome China's strong suit—its seemingly endless supply of infantrymen. There appeared to be little hope of matching these numbers with Americans, but there were others who wanted to fight the Communists in Korea—including some North Koreans. During the U.N. withdrawal, the Allies assisted thousands of anti-Communist northerners in escaping to islands off North Korea's coasts. On some of these islands, American officers armed the refugees with captured Communist weapons and created guerrilla units, units that might be employed against the Communists. Kim Yong Bok, the farmer who saw his family's land confiscated and fled to the mountains during the rule by the Communists, tells what happened after the Chinese had pushed U.N. forces out of North Korea:

". . . [After] the United Nations forces withdrew. . . . Again, I fled to hiding in the mountains . . . I was able to get food from the village because the enthusiastic Communists who had escaped, had not yet returned. Some of those who were caught in the village when the United Nations forces had overrun the province, had been executed by us. Therefore, most of the villagers were friendly, or at least not hostile to me. One day one of the villagers told me, in hiding, that the NKA troops had ordered them to repair a damaged boat at the beach, and the man told me about when the repairs would be finished. So, in February 1951, myself and another refugee came out to Cho-do (the suffix '-do' means 'island' in Korean) in that boat. . . .

"I knew the inhabitants of Cho-do were friendly because at that time ROK ships were taking refugees from our province to that island. From Cho-do I came down to

... **February 21, 1951.** General Ridgway initiates Operation KILLER, a major U.N. offensive.

Paengnyong-do on or about February 28, 1951. A week later, I met Major Burke, Commanding Officer of Leopard Base [the West Coast U.S. headquarters site for partisan support].

"I had not known Mr. Chang Sok Lin, who became the leader of Donkey 4. [The Americans had dubbed each of the North Korean guerrilla groups as a "Donkey" unit, differentiating them with a numerical designation.] When I arrived, I heard Mr. Chang was organizing a guerrilla group, so one night I called on him to join his unit. After

A gathering on the islands. Partisans and an American adviser in June 1951. Anti-Communist North Koreans flocked to their country's offshore islands when U.N. forces withdrew from the North. Eventually, the American Far East Command would arm, train, and direct some 22,000 of these northerners in conducting raids and intelligence missions behind Communist lines.

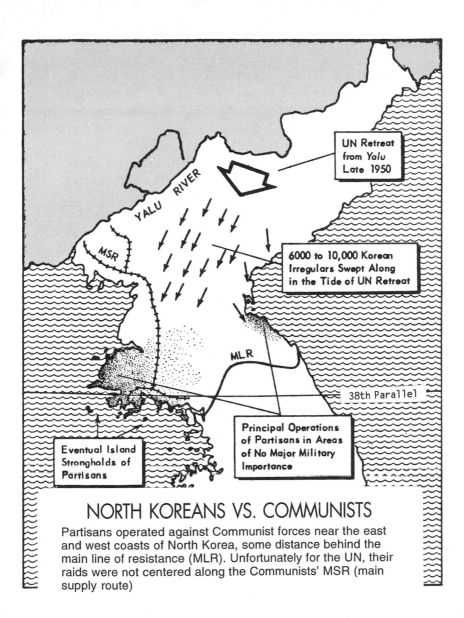

UN Retreat from *Yalu* Late 1950

6000 to 10,000 Korean Irregulars Swept Along in the Tide of UN Retreat

YALU RIVER

MSR

MLR

38th Parallel

Principal Operations of Partisans in Areas of No Major Military Importance

Eventual Island Strongholds of Partisans

NORTH KOREANS VS. COMMUNISTS

Partisans operated against Communist forces near the east and west coasts of North Korea, some distance behind the main line of resistance (MLR). Unfortunately for the UN, their raids were not centered along the Communists' MSR (main supply route) training was finished, twenty-six of us, including Mr. Chang, went to the mainland with a radio, ten carbines, one Russian light machinegun, thirty Russian rifles and some demolitions. It was March 5, 1951. This was the very beginning of my guerrilla life.

"Under the efficient command of Mr. Chang, we were able to stay in Pul-ta-san (a mountain on the west coast of North Korea) for about a month. During those days, we obtained information of the enemy in the region. Also I personally, leading four or five men, had made several attacks, surprising the enemy and killing them, capturing their weapons and food. I was permitted by Mr. Chang to be a member of Donkey 4 because I was just recently out of the province. Also, I had rescued quite a few loyal youths there and armed them with captured weapons. Soon after we began operations on the mainland our strength grew to approximately sixty men.

"One day, about 23 March 1951, early in the morning, I took five men with me and surprised eight NKA soldiers, including one master sergeant, who were supervising civilians digging trenches. . . . We captured the master sergeant and a private. Even though we had killed quite a few of the enemy by that time, they were our first prisoners. For the first time, we could get fresh and living information which accurately pictured the whole enemy situation. . . . From the information furnished by the prisoners, we first learned there were 4,000 NKA troops staying around the foot of Pul-ta-san. . . ."

Meanwhile, Ridgway's forces had been making steady, if costly, progress northward. On occasion, the Communists would launch a counterattack and the Allies would give ground. But the movement of the front was unmistakable. Day by day, it was shifting to the north. The Han was once again crossed, and on March 15 Seoul was in Allied hands yet one more time.

Taking Chinese fire. *Members of the 15th U.S. Infantry in action, March 23, 1951.*

Early in the next month, U.N. forces began crossing the 38th parallel in large formations. Indeed, under the steady and determined hand of its leader, the U.N. army had experienced a rebirth. Ridgway had brought about a renaissance.

Should the Allies continue north and once again attempt the liberation of North Korea? Should the war be extended if necessary? Among U.S. leaders, there was disagreement. The President, the Secretary of State, and the Joint Chiefs of Staff worked out a plan with America's allies to keep the conflict

---

... **March 14, 1951.** South Koreans reenter Seoul ... **March 25, 1951.** ROK patrols cross 38th Parallel heading north. . . . .

limited to the Korean Peninsula and negotiate an end to the war with the goal of achieving "a unified, independent and democratic state." This goal, of course, was precisely what the American and Soviet occupation authorities had argued about before the war, failing to agree on the meaning of the word "democratic." In Tokyo the U.S. Far East commander, General of the Army Douglas MacArthur, saw it differently. Suggesting Chiang Kai-shek's troops might be used in Korea and stating "there is no substitute for victory," the general twice violated one of President Truman's policies. With the support of his most trusted military and diplomatic advisers, the President relieved MacArthur of command on April 11 and selected Matthew B. Ridgway as the replacement.

6

PUNCH AND COUNTERPUNCH

April 11–November 27, 1951

THE FIRING of General of the Army Douglas MacArthur provided Americans a temporary, headlines-grabbing drama. The general's return to the United States was marked by an eloquent address to the Congress and a flurry of commentary about his chances for a presidential nomination, the latter fed by substantial public dissatisfaction with the conduct of the war. But popular enthusiasm for MacArthur faded when alternatives to the Truman policy were seriously examined. The Korean War was logically governed by the imperatives of a limited conflict. This was not a crusade that would demand all of the nation's

April 11, 1951. Truman fires MacArthur; Ridgway to succeed MacArthur, Lieutenant General James A. Van Fleet to succeed Ridgway . . . .

energy and dedication. Only a small portion of America's manpower, industrial might, and armed forces was engaged on that Asian peninsula. The U.S. had other security interests to attend to. The commonsense case for backing the President's restrained handling and discounting MacArthur's recommended and potentially dangerous approach was probably best spelled out by the general's successor, Ridgway:

"I thought the President had made it unmistakably clear that his primary concern was not to be responsible for initiating World War III. It was a clear recognition that I got through the message from JCS [the U.S. Joint Chiefs of Staff], not long after I arrived in Tokyo. . . . It said that the Soviet divisions in the Maritime Provinces [Soviet territory bordering on North Korea] were in an advanced stage of readiness for war and could initiate it with little or no warning. . . . My primary mission was the defense of Japan. . . . His [President Truman's] instructions to MacArthur were categoric, and in most cases, disregarded. . . . He [the President] did not want to start World War III. MacArthur had been pressing to attack China, to bring Chinese troops [the Nationalist troops of Chiang Kaishek, then based in Taiwan] into the Korean Peninsula, or to impose a blockade on the Chinese coast. . . .

"I consulted with JCS on this. For instance, MacArthur wanted to attack targets across the Yalu. Vandenberg [JCS member General Hoyt S. Vandenberg, Chief of Staff of the Air Force] was very much opposed to it. He said, 'If we do that now, our losses through attrition, plus combat, will so weaken us that we will not be able to respond or build up for two years thereafter in case something breaks out in Europe.' "

Ridgway knew Korea was neither the first nor the second strategic consideration for American leaders. At the time he

The Eighth Army commander, General James A. Van Fleet. Photograph taken in August 1951.

took MacArthur's place as the ranking U.S. military leader in the Far East, more American forces were being shipped to Europe than to Korea. Both Europe and Japan were regarded as being more important to Washington than Korea. If World War III did come, the United States must have the bulk of its forces in the right places.

Ridgway's replacement, General James Van Fleet, enjoyed the success of the offensive his predecessor had begun for only a few days. But the second foray of American forces north of the 38th parallel came to an abrupt halt with a large-scale Chinese offensive on April 22. Within a month, this attack would throw U.N. ground forces south of the parallel. When

. . . **April 22, 1951.** Communists launch spring offensive, knocking U.N. forces back below 38th Parallel on west and central fronts, but fail to recapture Seoul . . . .

the assault began, there was considerable danger that some of the American units, particularly units of the U.S. 3rd Division, might be cut off and trapped by the onrushing Chinese. By the second day of the offensive, the division had given up about ten miles of hard-won territory, but one of its infantry regiments, the 7th, was still too exposed—too far north. The Chinese had two battalions of the regiment under fire and were threatening to go south behind the Americans:

". . . the S-3 [operations officer] of the 1st Battalion called Mooney [Lieutenant Harley F. Mooney, A Company commander] to tell him the regiment had orders to move to a fortified Eighth Army line just north of Seoul.

" 'You and Baker Company are to cover the withdrawal of the 3rd Battalion and then be prepared to move Able Company out at 10 A.M.' . . .

"Lieutenant Mooney called his platoon leaders to tell them of the orders, then walked over to the top of Hill 283 to coordinate plans with the commander of Company B [Captain Ray W. Blandin, Jr.]. The time was about 8 A.M. . . .

"It had taken about two hours for two of the three companies to clear through Company A's area. In the meantime, Captain Blandin's Company B [unaware of the delay] had reached the bottom of the hill where he reported to his battalion commander [Lieutenant Colonel Frederick C. Weyand]. Colonel Weyand, realizing that the plans had miscarried, told him to get one platoon back on the top of the hill as quickly as possible to help Mooney hold his right flank.

"Lieutenant Eugene C. May [a Company B officer] turned his platoon around and started back up the hill. He was near the top of the trail at 11:30 A.M. When he arrived, the last company of the 3rd Battalion was strung out along the ridge top, and the entire company front was suddenly quiet. From the west end of the line Mooney called Lieu-

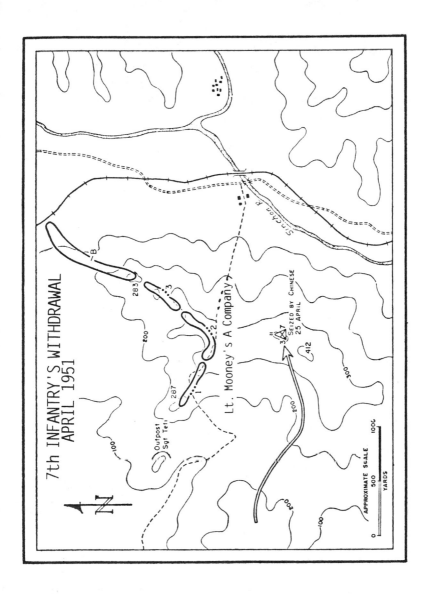

7th INFANTRY'S WITHDRAWAL
APRIL 1951

N

Lt. Mooney's A Company

Outpost
Sgt Tell

Seized by Chinese
25 April

Sinchon R

B

285

287

200

100

200

300

100

412

APPROXIMATE SCALE
0   500   1000
YARDS

97

tenant [John N.] Middlemas who was now watching the east end of the line. Mooney explained that all the firing at his end of the line had stopped, and asked what was happening on the opposite flank.

" 'It's so quiet here,' " said Middlemas, 'I'm just about ready to read some adventure stories for excitement.'

"At that instant there was the sound of scattered rifle fire from the top of Hill 283 where a sergeant and four men had been sent to outpost the right flank after Company B had vacated its sector. . . .

"Within a minute or two, the sergeant in charge of the outpost appeared, running . . . and yelling in a voice loud enough to be heard by the entire 3rd Platoon: 'They're coming! They're coming! Millions of them! They'll banzai us!'. . . At the same time, three of the infantrymen at that end of the line started to abandon their holes, fearing that the right flank was crumbling.

"Lieutenant Middlemas was yelling loudly and pounding several of the men on their helmets. 'Get the hell back in your positions! Get up on that damned hill!'

"He shoved the three men back in their holes, called to the 3rd Platoon to send up one squad immediately, and then started chasing the sergeant from the outpost and his four men back to the intermediate brush-covered knoll. They arrived there just in time to shoot one Chinese who was racing up the opposite side. There were ten to fifteen more enemy soldiers running from Hill 283 toward them. If the Chinese took this intermediate knoll they could fire down onto the top of the trail, severing the only route of withdrawal and evacuation. Lieutenant Middlemas knew he would have to hold off the Chinese for at least a half hour, or suffer heavy losses. He also knew they would probably either win or lose the battle within the next few minutes.

" 'Get to firing. Get to firing!' Middlemas shouted.

"The action on this end of the line developed fast. There was considerable enemy fire coming from Hill 283 and a few Chinese crept within grenade range before they were killed. Within another minute or two, however, an eight-man squad from the 3rd Platoon reached the knoll, making a total of fourteen men there, including Middlemas. All of them were firing rapidly.

"A platoon leader of Company D in charge of the two heavy machine guns with Company A saw the critical situation as it developed and rushed the heavy machine gun from the 3rd Platoon to the knoll. Then he sent for both the light caliber .30 and the heavy machine gun that were with the 2nd Platoon. All of this action had taken place within five minutes after the sergeant in charge of the outpost signaled the alarm.

"Up on the knoll the sergeant who had been in charge of the outpost had recovered his composure and was now reassuring his men. 'We're holding them! By God, we're holding them.'. . .

"One of the men started yelling, 'Come and get it!' and the other men took it up, either firing or screaming at the Chinese. Once, when their rate of fire dropped noticeably, there was a sudden increase in the amount of fire received from the Chinese. After that experience the Americans kept up a heavy volume of fire, and although Lieutenant Middlemas believed it was this sudden and heavy base of fire that was built up in the first ten minutes of the action that saved the flank, he was now concerned with making the ammunition last until everyone was off the hill. He went back and forth across his short line cautioning the men to fire aimed shots and hold down their rate of firing. . . .

"About 11:45 A.M. Mooney reached the area of activity. At that time the last of the 3rd Battalion was passing through Company A's area . . . Lieutenant Mooney got in touch [by radio] with his battalion commander, Colonel Weyand, to tell him of the situation and that he desperately needed some artillery support. . . .

"Colonel Weyand . . . called for artillery, gave them the general area, and asked for one round. Mooney reported that he could neither see nor hear this round, especially through the heavy firing going on where he was standing. Weyand then asked for a shift 'right 200, drop 200' and within a minute this round fell squarely on the enemy . . . there were loud screams from the Chinese.

"Mooney yelled over the radio, 'That's beautiful! That's beautiful! Fire for effect! Throw out some more!'. . .

"He ordered [the] men to move out one at a time, Indian fashion, with the men farthest from the trail moving first so that he would be able to keep men along the trail to protect it. This plan would also release the men in the order that they became least valuable. . . .

"Colonel Weyand kept urging Mooney to hurry since the artillery battery firing for him was almost out of shells. . . . Weyand arranged for an air strike and the planes soon appeared circling overhead until they could be called in. . . . after the artillery fire stopped. . . .

"Shortly after 12 P.M. Colonel Weyand again called, urging Mooney to 'move fast and get down from there.' Except for those men still firing at the Chinese, all men from Company A had cleared the top of the trail. Mooney asked for smoke to screen the movement of these men as they broke contact. With smoke and a mixture of explosive shells to replace the machine-gun and rifle fire, men from the last group started to leave—they needed no urging. Less than five minutes elapsed from the time the first of the forty-five left their position until the last was on the trail. As the last man left, the artillery fire stopped and the planes commenced the air strike.

"The entire action on the right flank had lasted from 11:30 A.M. until approximately 12:15 P.M. During this time two men had been killed by enemy rifle fire. When the tail of the column had gone about seventy-five yards down the trail, a single mortar round landed on the trail, killing one man and wounding four others, including Lieutenants Middlemas and Mooney, both of whom were hit in the leg by mortar fragments. By the time this happened a few Chinese were at the top of the trail and began firing down upon the withdrawing column. The last men in the column turned to fire up at the top of the trail, backing down the hill as they did so."

The U.N. offensive begun by Ridgway and continued by Van Fleet could not be sustained. There were simply too many Chinese foot soldiers coming south. How they did this in the face of overwhelming Allied air superiority was revealed by the testimony of a Communist prisoner who had traveled from China.

PRISONER: . . . we had to march only at night.

INTERVIEWER: What enemy weapons did the men in your unit talk about the most?

PRISONER: . . . The artillery, and the next was the airplane. The artillery was frightening because of its rapidity. Most frightening of what airplanes did was strafing.

INTERVIEWER: . . . How much of the march (down the Peninsula) was on foot? How much in vehicles of any sort?

PRISONER: We walked all the way down. We could never utilize any vehicle. Only the transportation unit could use the vehicles. . . .

INTERVIEWER: While traveling on the road, what measures did your unit take to avoid becoming seen and being surprised by enemy airplanes?

The thousand-yard stare. *Exhausted members of Company L, 7th U.S. Infantry after holding Hill 717 against an all-night Chinese assault. The vacant look on these survivors' faces, the result of extreme fatigue and shock, was often called the thousand-yard stare.*

PRISONER: When it snowed, we covered white cloths over us. If one had no white cloth, he wore the uniform inside out, because the inside of the uniform was white. Even under the moonlight, there was less possibility to be found by covering white cloths over us. When it wasn't snowing, we camouflaged with twigs and grass. For the equipment, artillery, machine guns, etc., it was the same.

INTERVIEWER: What warning system was used to alert units of approaching enemy aircraft?

PRISONER: Anyone who found it ahead was to notify orally that enemy planes were raiding. But sometimes, we had only one signal man in each Company who was to notify us by trumpet.

INTERVIEWER: How much time did you have between the warning and the time the airplane appeared?

PRISONER: Usually one or two minutes after such an alert was given, the enemy plane appeared above us. The way of alert was just blowing the trumpet two or three times regardless of the kind of airplanes.

INTERVIEWER: What did your group do when the alert was given or when planes were heard?

PRISONER: When we were on the highway, we scattered rapidly to make use of the natural features on both sides of the road. Once we took shelter, we would not move at all. While marching on the mountain path, we also spaced out rapidly and took shelter among the trees or rocks around there. If we didn't have time or place to do so, we just took shelter wherever we could and would not move at all. Under the moonlight, the way wasn't much different.

INTERVIEWER: Did your group stop or continue? Why?

PRISONER: We stopped marching at once and when the enemy plane disappeared completely, we continued marching. But if it was an especially dark night, or there was snow, we continued marching regardless—without stopping. On a very dark night, it seemed difficult to find us on the ground from the air. . . .

The difficulty in interdicting Communist supply lines during the day and the apparent impossibility to stem the nighttime flow of men and matériel from China by use of American airpower were recognized by a senior U.S. airman in 1951. A week prior to the April Chinese offensive, the U.S. Fifth Air Force commander, General Earl E. Partridge, stated:

"I believe that the paramount deficiency of the United States Air Force today—certainly as regards air-ground operations—is our inability to effectively seek out and destroy the enemy at night."

There was also an obvious problem in keeping the Communists from moving men and matériel south during the day. In order to begin afresh and make a special, coordinated effort in interdicting Chinese and North Korean movement, the U.S. Air Force launched "Operation Strangle" in May. Much of this scheme had to do with creating holes in roads with bombs, particularly in low-lying areas that were subject to springtime flooding. Another facet, of course, was aimed at knocking out bridges. And, since rail supply was such an efficient means to keep the Communist forces stocked with rice, ammunition, and clothing, the North Korean railway network was once again subjected to systematic air attack. Air Force Chief of Staff General Vandenberg explained:

"An important feature of Operation Strangle is its carefully planned regularity and the continuous pressure which it maintains. As you know, air attacks have been compared to the cavalry of the Civil War, which often disrupted supply lines for only brief periods. It was learned then that wars cannot be won merely by occa-sional hit-and-run strikes behind enemy lines, and this was all that cavalry forces could accomplish. Airpower, how-ever, because of its speed and flexibility, is capable of returning to the attack day after day and hour after hour. Against targets on the move, which are the only important targets we have left in Korea, it is essential to keep hitting

First Lieutenant James W. Enos and his B-26. This twin-engine bomber, known as the A-26 in World War II, was the workhorse of night air interdiction during the Korean War. Sometimes outfitted with searchlights on the wings, the nose-mounted armament of the plane could be devastating to a Communist convoy caught on the road. Enos was with the fifth U.S. Air Force, 3rd Bomber Group, stationed at Wakuni, Japan.

around the clock, every day, to prevent the concentrated movements during periods when the enemy is not under attack. When used in this manner, airpower is able to exert constant and destructive pressure on the enemy all the way back to his sources of supply. This destructive pressure from the air can be as relentless as the pressure exerted by our ground forces against his front-line troops. . . .

"Of course, an effort like Operation Strangle will not stop the enemy dead in his tracks. As long as he is willing to pay the price in transport vehicles and equipment destroyed, he may be able to maintain his armies in some degree of operational effectiveness on the front lines."

General Vandenberg's concluding caveat was understated. A few months after the operation had begun, it became painfully obvious that the interdiction campaign had not impeded the flow of Communist troops and supplies to the South. The Far East Air Force judged Operation Strangle a failure. The Communists simply enlisted a legion of peasants to repair roads and bridges within hours after they had been damaged or destroyed. And even if all of the planes in the entire U.S. inventory had been devoted to round-the-clock interdiction of North Korea's road system, there would never have been enough aircraft to continuously observe and strike all the routes the Communists could have used to support their ground operations. In and of itself, U.N. airpower was not capable of stopping or perhaps even significantly slowing down the Chinese and North Korean offensive. However, used in conjunction with U.N. ground troops, airpower was extremely effective, particularly when it was coordinated with well-placed artillery fire. It was the combination of determined U.N. infantrymen defending their ground, assisted by superior firepower—rifles, machine guns, and artillery—and the air-delivered bombs, rockets, and

Thief's end in a "police action." *An American infantryman from the 5th Infantry views the body of a Chinese soldier wearing GI undergarments and carrying an American magazine. Early 1951.*

napalm that stopped the spring 1951 Communist offensive short of Seoul.

By early May the Allies' counterattack had recovered most of the lost ground. In mid-May the Communists struck again and U.N. forces fell back. But in late May General Van Fleet's ground forces began a steady march against a played-out adversary. Eighth Army estimated the Chinese and North Koreans had suffered over 200,000 casualties from April to June. U.N. progress was initially rapid. Then, as the Allies reached a maximum advance, fifty miles north of the 38th parallel, resistance stiffened and U.S. and ROK losses mounted. Finally, the Soviet delegate at the United Nations suggested cease-fire discussions begin. Secretary of State Dean Acheson spoke of this in his New York City talk:

"This brings me to the armistice negotiations. On June 23, 1951, Jacob Malik, who was then Soviet Union representative on the [U.N.] Security Council, made a radio address here in New York. In the course of it he said this:

' "The Soviet peoples believe that the most acute problem of the present day, the problem of the armed conflict in Korea, could also be settled. The Soviet peoples believe that, as a first step, discussions should be started between the belligerents for a cease-fire and an armistice providing for the mutual withdrawal of forces from the 38th parallel."

"That seemed to be a pretty important announcement by a power which had a pretty direct relation to this matter in Korea and, of course, a great deal of attention was paid to it. Immediately, the United States Ambassador in Moscow called on Mr. Gromyko [Andrei Gromyko, the Soviet Foreign Minister] and asked for clarification of this state-

. . . **June 3, 1951.** U.S. supported partisan operations begin along North Korea's east coast.

ment by Mr. Malik. Mr. Gromyko explained that, in his view, the armistice should, in the first place, include a cease-fire and, secondly, should be limited to strictly military questions without involving any political or territorial matters. That seemed pretty hopeful; that seemed to be a sensible way of getting at the matter. So General Ridgway immediately established contact with the Communist Command, and arrangements were made to initiate negotiations.

"I shall go through some of those steps . . . it is quite important to try to see what the United Nations Command was attempting to do. It had three main purposes in mind. The first one was to try to bring an end to the fighting on a basis which achieves the purpose of repelling the aggression. That was essential. . . .

"Secondly, the purpose was to get the maximum possible assurance against a renewal of the fighting. . . .

"Thirdly, the purpose was to bring about a fair exchange of prisoners."

The first talks were held at Kaesong, very close to the 38th parallel, on July 10, 1951. A casual observer might have concluded that the Communists would have done well to agree to the best deal they could wrangle from the Allies and quickly sign a cease-fire agreement. After all, the air- and seapower advantage was decidedly with the U.N. And, during July, the Allied ground contingent counted 554,577 men: 253,250 Americans, 273,266 South Koreans, and 28,061 troops from several U.N. member nations. The number of Communist ground forces, on the other hand, was slightly lower, totaling 459,200: 248,100 Chinese and 211,100 North Koreans. But these numbers were deceiving. The numbers of American

---

June 23, 1951. Soviet U.N. delegate, Jacob A. Malik, proposes cease-fire talks . . . **July 10, 1951.** Military armistice negotiations begin at Kaesong. . . . .

ground troops included a huge proportion of logistical, medical, transportation, and support units, necessary to the American way of fighting on land. And the ROK numbers were still mainly composed of ill-trained, ill-equipped refugees that had been swept up in the disastrous retreat of a year before. In reality, the Communists had far more fighting men on the front lines than did the Allies.

In the face of this roughly even balance in combat power, the discussions produced little more than propaganda and a reduced level of fighting. While combat between the regulars became less mobile and intense, both sides dug a well-defined, extensive system of opposing trenches on the mountains and across the valleys of the Peninsula. Meanwhile, from the spring until the fall of 1951, another kind of war, the one behind the Communist lines, became more active and wide-ranging. Several thousand U.S.-advised, -armed, and -trained North Korean guerrillas expanded their operations. Kim Yong Bok's experience during 1951 was typical:

"Taking the twelve men and radio, I organized a new unit with thirty-six men. On May 27, 1951, we landed in Hwanghae province and went to Pak-sok-san (the same mountain where Kim had fought before), where we set up our base. . . . We started sending to headquarters information about supplies and enemy positions, and ambushing the enemy on the roads. Thus we guerrillas harassed the enemy almost every day.

"For instance, on 25 June 1951, Mr. Kim Jun Gol, my adjutant, surprised an enemy police station detachment at Un-Yu-myon with ten men and again on 14 July 1951, I myself with ten men surprised the enemy at Song-ha-on-

An unlikely landing craft. *Partisans used fishing junks common to the coasts of North Korea to begin their raids from the offshore islands. These sometimes included concealed recoilless rifles on the decks and high-speed diesel engines for hasty escapes.*

chon. A few days later we had a little misfortune. My radio broke down on July 21 and communications between me and Donkey 4 was cut off, and supplies had stopped because the communications through which we had been supported by our headquarters were cut off. I could receive messages from headquarters but not transmit them. . . . Having even one-sided contact with headquarters kept us of peaceful mind and we decided that before we left we would get in another attack. . . . Regrettably, while we were planning a surprise, the enemy finally discovered us and I lost three of my good men. These were the first men I had lost.

"After receiving some supplies by liaison group [the

American advisers] from Donkey 4 headquarters, we came out [from the mainland] to Cho-do [a guerrilla-held island] on July 26, 1951. When I met my leader, Mr. Chang, I suggested it was wise to have our base on Cho-do rather than to have all the people in the mountains during the coming rainy season. Secondly, we needed some people to stay in the rear and replace the people on the mainland. Another reason, we needed to have an island base near to our operations area. The leader, Chang, agreed with me, and we also had permission at Leopard Base [the west-coast American guerrilla support headquarters] to have Cho-do as the base for Donkey 3. I had increased my strength as well as equipment up to two hundred and started operating from Cho-do.

"By that time, Mr. Chang had four hundred people under him. He was operating from his island quite actively and he and I were competing as to which unit would produce better results in operations. Both units were doing an excellent job as guerrillas, destroying enemy installations, cutting their railroad tracks, ambushing them on roads, and destroying bridges. A comparatively big operation was performed by myself when I led fifteen men to attack Yul-ti-myon.

"When I increased my strength to two hundred, I had several groups of armed people which were not a part, until that time, of any particular organization. One of those groups was led by Mr. Chong Song Yong. He had twenty-six men under him. Mr. Chong Song Yong later became my chief of staff.

"Also, on 29 July 1951, with forty people I had assaulted one enemy company in Pung-chon early in the morning . . . at that time, I had captured three sail junks from the mainland. With some other sail junks borrowed from the civilians on my location, I had landed on the mainland very often. Particularly in the autumn I per-

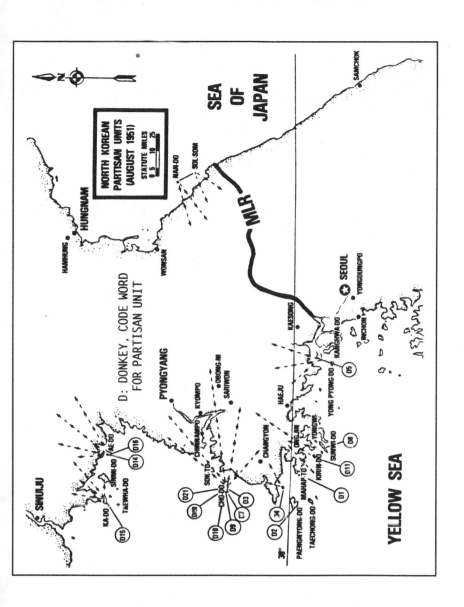

113

Partisans training partisans. *American advisers not only trained North Korean guerrillas, they trained guerrilla instructors as well so that their northern allies would become as self-sufficient as possible. Here a guerrilla instructs recruits in the operation of an American-made recoilless rifle.*

formed operations almost every day. It was the best season to attack the enemy harvest spot tax [North Korean troops collected rice, animal, and other in-kind taxes each fall from the peasantry] and to capture enemy ox-carts fully loaded with spot tax grain. We destroyed the oxcarts, capturing the oxen as well as the spot tax material.

"Chill Bong San (in the Korean language, 'seven peaks mountains') was my secret base. One of my agents on the mainland one day asked me to move a whole village to Cho-do where they could find safety. Despite receiving some resistance from the enemy, we moved 23 families with more than 140 people, including children and very aged people, to Cho-do. It was a great labor to escort the 140 people including those infants and aged people all the way to Cho-do."

Another Donkey team leader, Lee Jung Hok, had similar experiences during the spring and summer of 1951 with Donkey 11, but noted a reversal of fortune in the fall:

"[From] Chang-lin-do, the battalion had performed an operation in the Song-gang area . . . on 17 June 1951. Seventy of the battalion participated in the operation; they killed about twenty enemy and captured one POW alive. There was another operation performed in the Yong-ho-do area. No-ho-ri, which is located across from Yong-ho-do, was attacked by thirty men of the battalion. . . . This operation lasted for about thirty days. During these days, the friendly [forces] had been staying in the mountains. In this one-month operation, we captured eighteen NKA and we killed a little more than fifty. . . .

"I had been having difficulties with the fact that there were too many people in my unit whom I was not able to feed. Therefore in September 1951, I had selected about 600 people among the 1,700 people as my unit. First of all I selected those people who did not have any families to support. Secondly, I selected the ones who already had combat experience, thirdly, I selected students, high school boys. Those of the 1,700 who were not chosen to remain guerrillas were given the choice of staying on the island or going south [to UN-occupied South Korea]. I divided the 600 [remaining armed guerrillas] into two Battalions. One was called the West Battalion and the other was called the East Battalion. . . .

"Early in November 1951, Cha-do was attacked and captured by the enemy. Cha-do was an important point for the transmission of intelligence . . . this was the first move in a campaign to drive us from the islands. Next the enemy attacked Shin-do. In the Shin-do operation, fifty or sixty enemy soldiers were killed and nine of us were killed. . . . We retreated to Yong-ho-do."

While the partisans were fighting behind North Korean and Chinese lines, a gradually increasing air-to-air campaign was being waged over their heads. The northwestern part of North Korea became known as MiG Alley, a place where U.S. bombers were now having to be escorted because of the growing numbers of Soviet-built jet fighters sent up to contest the raids. Initially, the Americans had the advantage. Flying F-86 Sabres, U.S. Air Force fighter pilots usually made short work of any Communist pilot who dared to come across the Yalu. On May 21 the Americans were able to claim their first jet ace, an F-86 pilot who had downed five enemy aircraft. That day, Sabre pilot Captain James Jabara was debriefed after scoring not only his fifth but his sixth MiG "kill" the day before. Jabara was debriefed by Colonel J. Meyer:

JABARA: Colonel Hinton called [on the radio] and said he saw many "bandits," MiGs coming across the river [the Yalu]. Just as soon as we made landfall [coming in from the sea], we were ordered to drop our tanks [wing-mounted external fuel tanks]. Right after we got inland, I saw about twelve MiGs. They saw us and made a pass at us.

MEYER: Where were they?

JABARA: They were above us, Colonel, they had just come across the river. We were at 27,000 feet [altitude], they were approximately at 30,000. They made a head-on pass at us. Two of them fired, they overshot and we turned around at 'em, tried to get on their tail. I never could get my right tank

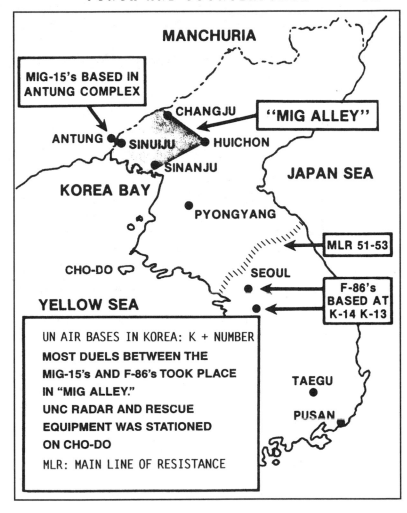

MANCHURIA

MIG-15's BASED IN
ANTUNG COMPLEX

CHANGJU

"MIG ALLEY"

ANTUNG SINUIJU HUICHON

SINANJU

KOREA BAY

JAPAN SEA

PYONGYANG

MLR 51-53

CHO-DO SEOUL

F-86's
BASED AT
K-14 K-13

YELLOW SEA

UN AIR BASES IN KOREA: K + NUMBER
MOST DUELS BETWEEN THE
MIG-15's AND F-86's TOOK PLACE
IN "MIG ALLEY."
UNC RADAR AND RESCUE
EQUIPMENT WAS STATIONED
ON CHO-DO
MLR: MAIN LINE OF RESISTANCE

TAEGU

PUSAN

off. [Jabara would be hampered during the entire action by
having a wing tank that he could not jettison, making his
F-86 slower and difficult to handle.] It sort of screwed me.
Three more came at us, made a pass at about 5 o'clock [from
Jabara's right rear].

MEYER: Now there were twelve of them, how many did you have?

JABARA: Two of us. Initially when we saw 'em, our whole flight broke up. When these three overshot us, we turned and broke into them. So, I latched on to the third man—he was straggling quite a bit. We went around and around.

MEYER: What altitude were you then?

JABARA: We started at 28,000 feet and ended up at about 25,000.

MEYER: You still had a tank on?

JABARA: Yes, sir. So, I got in range and started shooting at him. On the second burst, I saw a . . . sort of looked like a flash fire. It was right below the cockpit, at the wing roots and all over the left wing. It just burst into flames. He did two snap rolls. My wing man called and said he saw fire. Then [the MiG] went into a spin. I could see him all the time because he was trailing smoke, heavy black smoke. I watched it. I thought he was going right in. But at about 10,000 feet the airplane leveled out just for a minute and I saw the pilot bail out. The airplane just exploded. Like when you get a good skeet shot—it just powders. It just fell to the ground. I don't think there was a big piece of it left at all. I made a pass at the pilot with my cameras. I had to get down for two or three seconds to get the camera switch and almost hit him. I had to pull up. He was twirling around like mad—dressed in black.

MEYER: Was he still in the seat?

JABARA: No, sir, just the parachute. I don't know what happened to the seat. He landed about five miles from where the airplane hit. After that, I was at about 7,000 feet and my wingman lost me. . . . I didn't know where he was. And I saw six more MiGs. Four of them flying a fingertip formation. Two sort of in trail—like another element.

MEYER: What altitude?

JABARA: They were at 20,000 feet. I had just pulled up. They were in a left turn and it was sort of a temptation to latch on to them. I started to shoot at the number six man. The other four people dove down. The number six man just climbed straight ahead. His element leader, with a flight of five—I figured he would be coming back at me. So, I was keeping a good eye out for him—trying to. [The one I was following] was up, higher than me but all the sudden he dove down to the left. I had no trouble catching up with him. I started shooting at him. I got several strikes. I don't know whether he was on fire or if he flamed out. ["Flameout," or a stoppage of combustion and resultant loss of power, was a common problem with the early jet engines.] He was pouring a lot of white smoke out his tail pipe. I overshot him right away. I looked around to see if there was anybody around on my tail. He started a turn—well, sort of a spiral—half spin, half spiral to the left. I put on my speed breaks [hinged surfaces on the fuselage that when extended into the slipstream would create drag and slow the aircraft] and turned around to watch him. I knew he was in trouble. I wanted to see if he was going to hit. I followed him down to about 6,500 feet. I think he was on fire, but I'm not sure because he was smoking like mad. He had flamed out, going slow. I was going at only about 170 knots, in a glide.

And, all of the sudden, there was popping all around me. MiGs were back there—shooting at me. I broke real hard to the left, as hard as I could. I pulled in the breaks and put on full power. I straightened it out after my initial break. But I couldn't do much more than 500 knots because it was too hard to control. I had to use both hands on the stick. It wanted to dip down to the left, I guess because of the tank. Every time I would straighten out, they would shoot at me. I could hear it before I could see it. It was pink—reddish pink. [Jabara was talking about the color of the tracer bullets. Normally, every fifth bullet would have a tracer element allowing the firer to adjust his aim.]

So, right then, Pitts [one of Captain Jabara's squadron

mates] called and said [on the radio], "There's an F-86 down there getting bounced by two MiGs."

I said, "I know it!"

Pitts says, "Who's the pilot?"

I must have been in a ten-G turn, so I holler, "Jaaabbbaaar-rraa." I kept breaking, building up my air speed and braking again. Pitts came down and started firing at the MiGs. They took off. I ended up at about 4,000 feet. I looked up and couldn't find the MiGs so I came on home.

The increasing air actions became a subject of conversation at the truce negotiations. The talks between the belligerents were becoming more acrimonious and hopes for a cease-fire began to dim. During the course of one exchange in early August, Lieutenant General Nam Il, the chief North Korean delegate, made a comment to the American representatives that was only later judged to have had significance:

"I would like to tell you frankly that in fact without direct support of your tactical aerial bombing alone, your ground forces would have been completely unable to hold their present positions. It is owing to your strategic air effort of indiscriminate bombing of our area, rather than to your tactical air effort of direct support to the front line, that your ground forces are able to maintain barely and temporarily their present positions."

This somewhat confusing statement contained a hidden preview of coming events. On the face of it, the North Korean general first gave a vote of confidence in the prowess of the U.N.'s tactical airpower. Then his praise was directed at Allied strategic bombing, an effort he apparently believed to be more potent than the U.N.'s tactical air capabilities. Whatever General Nam Il's meaning, it could not be interpreted as being respectful of U.N. ground forces and it came at a time of

The MiG buster. *The North American F-86 Sabre first flew in 1947 and rapidly became one of the most capable swept-wing fighters of the midcentury. Armed with six 50-caliber machine guns and capable of speeds of over 600 miles per hour, the plane gave an excellent account of itself in air-to-air combat during the Korean War.*

growing impasse in the joint discussions. As the lack of progress became apparent in August 1951, the talks were suspended and General Van Fleet mounted a series of limited, ground-gaining offensives designed to drive the Communists back to the negotiating table. For the most part, the criticized U.N. ground forces were successful in their drive against the Communist ground forces.

Then the North Koreans suddenly resorted to a new-style offensive of their own: a surge in air-to-air combat. For some months, particularly since Jabara's stunning feat, American airmen had few tangles with Soviet-built MiG-15 fighter jets. Largely, victories by the Communist pilots were over U.S. propeller-driven bombing planes. But when the U.S. Air Force and U.S. Navy began regular patrolling of the northern reaches of North Korea with high-performance fighters, the MiGs began disappearing—under the guns of the superior American pilots, and by a noticeable Communist reluctance to take on American airmen. However, on the first day of September, an all-out MiG offensive campaign was launched, staged by Communist pilots and an inventory of MiGs that had grown to over five hundred airframes. This campaign was apparently what the Communist negotiator, Lieutenant General Nam Il, had been hinting at: a maximum effort to clear the skies of U.S. bombers and their escorting fighters. If it succeeded, and if the general's analysis about the effect of American airpower was correct, the Communists would undoubtedly throw the U.N. ground forces off the Peninsula. Years after this surprising offensive, an American Air Force veteran, armed with evidence that only came to light well after the fight, described the "North Korean" airmen and the restrictions on American airmen. General William W. "Spike" Momyer said:

"Of course the NKAF (North Korean Air Force) was not all Korean, but basically Chinese with Russian and Polish pilots as well. Further, there is substantial reason to believe that most of the fighter squadrons actively engaging the F-86s were Soviet squadrons being rotated through the front at about six-week intervals.

"General Otto Weyland, Commander of the Far East Air Force, stated that the first priority of his air force was to keep the air force in North Korea neutralized so that the NKAF could not attack Allied ground forces. There were seventy-five airfields in North Korea that could have supported MiG-15s. During the course of the war, these air fields were suppressed by the combined efforts of Fifth Air Force and Far East Air Force Bomber Command.

"The enemy sanctuary in China greatly compounded our problems in maintaining air superiority, of course, for we could neither destroy MiGs on the ground at their Chinese bases nor follow them into Chinese air space to destroy them in the air. We dealt with the situation primarily through the use of fighter sweeps and screens. Fighter sweeps were commonly used as they had been in World War II, to entice the enemy to come up for battle. These sweeps were made in areas such as MiG Alley where the probability of engagement was high. The frequency and size of the sweeps depended on the availability of our fighters, the probability of enemy reaction and the supporting effect such flights would have on other operations. Other F-86 patrols along the Yalu screened the fighter-bombers conducting attacks against the rail network and other targets associated with the enemy's logistical system. The F-86s by interposing themselves between the fighter-bombers and the MiG-15s based in the Antung area, allowed [other aircraft] to carry out their missions with almost complete security."

The Communist air offensive of September 1951 was described by U.S. Air Force Lieutenant Colonel Robert F. Futrell:

". . . the Communist air forces launched into a bitter and all-out air campaign on September 1, 1951. Why the Reds selected this date for mounting their air offensive was easily surmised. On August 23, truce talks had broken down at Kaesong, and since August 18, FEAF [Far East Air Force] fighter-bombers had been hammering North Korea's railway lines. . . . As many as 90 MiG's now entered North Korea at one time, and with so many aircraft in the skies, the Reds employed practically any formation they desired. In aerial fights on September 8 and 9, the MiG pilots showed tactics never before seen in Korea. Some MiG's attacked in trail, others used the lufbery circle, while in one instance four flights of MIG's flew line-abreast head-on passes in which all sixteen planes blazed at a single Sabre. The latter tactic puzzled the Sabre pilots, but Colonel Gabreski, an expert on Luftwaffe tactics, recognized that the Reds were employing a technique which the Germans had used against B-17 formations in World War II. All hostile air formations were tighter and better organized. One formation was particularly hard to combat. Pools of MiG's orbited at superior altitudes waiting to make passes downward at United Nations aircraft which came within range. After diving down and making firing passes, the MiG's zoomed back upstairs.

"During September 1951 4th Fighter-Interceptor Wing pilots sighted 1,177 MiG sorties over North Korea and engaged 911 of the MiG's in combat. Considering that they commonly fought at odds of three or four to one against them, the Sabre pilots gave good account of themselves. Shortly after noon on September 2, for example, 22 Sabres tangled with 40 MiG's in a thirty-minute air battle which raged between Sinuiju and Pyongyang and resulted in the destruction of four MiG's. Again, on the afternoon of September 9, 28 Sabres opposed 70 MiG's, and in this air battle Captains Richard S. Becker and Ralph D. Gibson each destroyed one of the Communist jet fighters, thus becoming the second and third jet air aces of the Korean conflict. In the course of September's all-out air battles, the Sabres destroyed 14 Red MiG's, and on 19 September a 49th Group Thunderjet pilot, Captain Kenneth L. Skeen, jettisoned his bombs and shot down an intercepting MiG.

...**August 23, 1951.** Communists break off talks charging U.S. planes violated Kaesong's neutrality...

In air-to-air engagements the Fifth Air Force lost three F-86's, one F-51, one F-80, and one F-84. While losses to Communist interceptors were moderate, the MiG's were seriously impeding the progress of the United Nations railway interdiction campaign. On many days the MiG's evaded Sabre patrols and pounced on the fighter-bombers, who had no recourse except to jettison their bombs, to scatter, and to run for their lives.

"Alarmed by the developments in Korea on 15 September, General Weyland frankly warned General Vandenberg that the Communist air force was rapidly getting out of control. The Red MiG's were hampering United Nations air-to-ground attacks as far southward as Pyongyang. General Weyland stated that FEAF had a "vital and immediate" requirement for another wing of Sabrejets. If the USAF could not provide the wing, Weyland recommended that one of FEAF's F-80 wings should be converted to F-86's. 'If the present trend continues,' Weyland warned, 'there is a definite possibility that the enemy will be able to establish bases in Korea and threaten our supremacy over the front lines.' In Washington General Vandenberg had serious concern over the increasing Communist air strength in Manchuria, but his operations officer informed him that the USAF could neither provide nor support FEAF with any more F-86's without seriously impairing the effectiveness of the Air Defense Command [the command responsible for defending the United States against the long-range Soviet bomber fleet]. 'Our present capability of supporting one F-86 unit in FEAF is questionable,' Vandenberg was told, 'and the ability to support two does not exist.' Aside from its inability to provide and support more Sabres in combat, USAF operations felt that no number of additional fighter units could assure air superiority in Korea unless the source of the enemy's air supplies could be attacked. On the basis of this precis,

General Vandenberg informed Weyland on September 20 that the USAF could neither provide nor support additional Sabre squadrons in Korea."

The limits for a limited war were being reached. Weyland did eventually get more Sabres when the MiG threat became even more serious in the next few months. But the U.S. Air Force was reaching a ceiling on what could be sent to Korea. America's air leaders had to consider the needs for the defense of Europe and the American homeland, both of which were considered more vital to U.S. interests than the distant Asian peninsula. It was the same for the U.S. Army. New ground combat units for General Van Fleet's efforts were becoming few and far between. On the other side of the line, the influx of Chinese continued, but not at the rate of increase the Allies had seen in early and mid-1951.

There was another limit on U.S. ground forces. Fighting during this period, the fall of 1951, was especially primitive for the Americans because they could not fully employ the advantages that the world's greatest industrial power was supposed to bring to a combat contest. An officer of the 2nd Infantry Division's 38th Infantry Regiment said it best when he spoke of a tough October action against the North Koreans:

"This battle is an especially interesting one to analyze since it reduced to a minimum the usual advantages which the American soldier enjoys over the Communist. More than anywhere else in the experience of this regiment, it pitted man against man. The great advantages accruing from our superior mobility (and this includes the use of tanks) were absent. To get to the line of departure, you dismount from a vehicle at the near side of the mountain

. . . **October 25, 1951.** Truce negotiations resumed at Panmunjom . . . .

ridge, climb steadily for two hours to a height of 1,148 meters, and then for two more hours climb up and down the rough, rocky trail to Hill 1179. Upon arriving at the line of departure, you are sure that you have done a good day's work, and indeed you have. For a man has to be in good physical shape to make it at all. Every round of ammunition, every ration, and every casualty had to be transported over this same rough and tortuous footpath. That it takes another four hours of climbing to cover the remaining 6,000 yards (straight-line distance) to the objective makes it clear that this was a battle requiring great physical exertion. In this respect, the fact that the men had seen forty days of continuous fighting up to this point had its advantages. It is also at once obvious that supply was the governing criterion. To compound the difficulty, this was a battle in which the North Korean resisted stubbornly, at times fanatically. In most cases he had to be killed in his cave, which he had hewn out of solid rock.

"Since terrain prohibited the employment of tanks in the fight, the tanks were immobilized and the tankers used both as supervisors over the Korean carriers and as pack-carriers themselves. To further help meet the carrying deficit, the attached AAA (Anti-aircraft Artillery) battery was employed the same way, as were all available personnel from Service and Headquarters Companies. The Medical Company could not be tapped, predictions being that it would have its hands full. Neither was the Mortar Company levied upon. Desirous of employing the maximum fire power possible, the Mortar Company was allowed to do its own hand-carrying of ammunition in order to supply the largest number of mortars it could thus support. This turned out to be one mortar, which later delivered over eight hundred rounds every day. It goes without saying that the best FO (forward observer) and the best gunners were used. The mortarmen carriers saw to it that every round of ammunition scored against the enemy.

"Air support played a negligible role in this attack. In this type of terrain it was found that strafing was of practically no value, rocketing of limited value, and napalm the only really effective weapon. . . ."

Van Fleet's steady but bloody progress northward, the limits on what both sides were now willing to put into the war, and the approach of another bitter cold Korean winter caused the belligerents to return to the negotiating table in November. Heretofore, the limits for both sides involved the amount of manpower and matériel each side would allocate to the war. The Americans, of course, had a self-imposed additional limit—there would be no use of their most powerful weapons, nuclear bombs. But there would be yet one more limit that would be approached. As the snows and increasingly frigid gusts of air arrived from Manchuria, the matter of endurance became important. Which side would be the first to yield, agreeing to terms favorable to the other side?

TALK-FIGHT, FIGHT-TALK

November 28, 1951–October 30, 1952

HOPES THAT THE Communists had returned their military delegates to the negotiation table in order to work out the terms of the cease-fire gradually diminished. Although they never said as much, as the months of negotiations ground on it became obvious that the Soviets, Chinese, and North Koreans believed they could achieve through negotiations what they could not win on the battlefield. From the beginning of 1951 until the July truce talks began, U.N. forces were fighting their way northward at the rate of about eight to ten miles per month. But when talks began in July, U.N. attacks all but stopped. Then, when

November 28, 1951. False rumors of cease-fire spread throughout the front, fighting virtually stops, then resumes. . . . .

On the way back up the peninsula. *Soldiers of the 5th U.S. Infantry in the attack. By 1952 a pattern of U.N. attacks during lulls in the negotiations and Communist attacks during active negotiations had been established.*

the Communists withdrew from the talks in late August, the U.N. advance resumed, averaging about five miles per month. Then, too, from November 1951 until April 1952, a period when the talks were once again in progress, both sides added to their strength, but the Communists added much more. U.N. strength grew about 10 percent while the Communists added fully 22 percent to their ranks. The Communists almost certainly concluded that the U.N. side wanted peace more than they did and that they were better off talking and fighting than fighting without talking.

At first, in 1951, American political and diplomatic leaders seemed unaware of the Communist talk-fight strategy, but as they realized what had happened, they began to search for a solution. Perhaps because they were closer to the scene, American military negotiators in Korea, men who were actually conducting the talks, became cognizant of the Communist scheme sooner than did U.S. diplomats. When Secretary of State Dean Acheson described the course of negotiations in late 1952, he still appeared to be incredulous about the delays caused by the Communists and unable to understand why the talks should be taking so long:

"On the military demarcation line, it took four months to get agreement. The Communist attitude was that the demarcation line should be the 38th parallel, although they had previously stated that the 38th parallel ceased to exist, although Mr. Gromyko had said that purely military and not political questions ought to be involved in this. Nevertheless, the Communists spent four months arguing that it should be the 38th parallel. The United Nations Command took the view that the 38th parallel had no military significance whatsoever, that the line must be based on the actual military situation and that it must be a line which left both sides in a defensible position. Finally, this was agreed to on November 27, 1951. . . .

"All sorts of political questions were introduced by the Communists. . . . The United Nations Command took the position that it was not able to discuss political questions

... **December 18, 1951.** Communist and U.N. negotiators exchange lists of prisoners of war. . . . .

of any sort. Finally, after a great effort, the agreement was [made] on a recommendation that a political conference on a higher level of both sides [was to] be held three months after an armistice was to become effective to settle through negotiations the questions of the withdrawal of all foreign forces from Korea, the peaceful settlement of the Korean question, etcetera. In agreeing to this recommendation, the United Nations Command negotiator stated that so far as the Command was concerned, the recommendation [was] directed to the United Nations as well as the Republic of Korea; that is, that the United Nations has a stake in the future settlement of these questions; that 'foreign forces' meant all non-Korean forces, and finally that the mystic word 'etcetera' should not be construed to relate to matters outside of Korea. They then took up the arrangements for a cease fire and for the supervision of a cease fire; and whereas the demarcation zone discussion had taken four months, this one took five months.

"The only purpose of United Nations Command under this item was to get the maximum assurance against a renewal of aggression. Therefore, at all times, the United Nations negotiators stood by these principles. In the first place, they were quite willing to have the same supervision, the same restrictions imposed on them as they asked should be imposed on the other side. There was never a departure from complete reciprocity of treatment. Therefore, the same limitations and arrangements behind the United Nations lines were to be accepted as on the other side. Secondly, they insisted that there should be no increase in the strength of the armed forces on either side but that there should be provision for the rotation of person-

... **January 24, 1952.** General Ridgway announces truce talks stalemated because of Communist demands for forcible repatriation of prisoners..............................

nel. You could not add to the strength, but you could change people, so that people that had been there a long time would not have to remain there indefinitely, and their places could be taken by others.

"In the third place, they insisted, on the United Nations Command's side, that the impartial commission must have free access to the territory of both sides to observe how the armistice was being observed. They were not willing to take the word of the other side. This had to be observed by impartial observers.

"The Communists continually referred to principles which caused a great deal of trouble. One of these principles was the freedom of their internal affairs from interference, which came up every time anybody suggested that anything should be done behind their lines, or that there should be an interference in the internal affairs of their country—whether it was that the airfield should not be repaired, or what not. That principle of course was a very troublesome one.

"They refused to agree that the airfields should not be reconstructed and rehabilitated. Another matter which took a very long time was that it had been agreed that there might be impartial nations nominated by each side on this inspection commission, provided that no side had a right to nominate a country which was offensive or not regarded as impartial by the other side. Therefore, when the United States suggested that Sweden, Switzerland and Norway should be impartial nations satisfactory to it, the Communists named Poland, Czechoslovakia and the Soviet Union. The presence of any of these nations as impartial ones was, of course, ridiculous, but the presence of the

---

... **January 31, 1952.** Communist attacks on partisan-held west-coast islands intensify ....

Soviet Union which, as I pointed out, had organized, equipped, advised, directed and trained and maintained this aggression, on a group of impartial observers was intolerable, and that could not be accepted.

"Finally, the negotiations got down to three points: the airfields, the question of the impartial nations and the treatment of prisoners. At that point, the United Nations Command put forward what was called a package proposal; that is, a proposal which would settle all three of these things at once. The proposal was that the United Nations Command would give up its insistence that the airfields should not be rehabilitated. It would withdraw that position provided it was agreed on the other side that the impartial group—the so-called supervision group—which is a better name for it—should be Sweden, Switzerland, Poland and Czechoslovakia, and that the United Nations position on prisoners of war should be accepted. That was the package deal which was put forward, and it was rejected.

"From that time on, the discussion revolved around the prisoner-of-war position. . . ."

By March 1952 the war had become static, but fighting and the casualties it caused continued. There was simply little movement on the ground. The battlefield increasingly resembled the Western Front of World War I, albeit a rather hilly replica. Trenches, bunkers, and sandbagged, seemingly permanent positions abounded. In spots behind the U.N. lines, metal Quonset huts began replacing tents. Much of the fighting revolved around making marginal geographic improvements in

... **February 18, 1952.** Major Communist prisoner rioting out on Koje island; U.N. guards kill 75 prisoners ... **February 19, 1952.** Agreement reached by both sides calling for high-level political conference to follow military-arranged truce. . . **March 1, 1952.** Tempo of U.N. partisan raids intensifies with improving weather. . . . .

one's lines—securing an advantage—maybe a slightly higher piece of ground so as to look down on the enemy instead of being exposed to his view. Hills and high spots along the entrenched, 120-mile-long front line, ones that had been referred to in the early stages of the war by their numerical elevations, were soon nicknamed by the Americans.

One of these was named Outpost Eerie, possibly because the GIs found it a spooky spot to defend. It was a platoon-size position halfway between the Chinese lines and those of the 45th U.S. Infantry Division. Eerie was only 120 feet above the valley floor. The American and Chinese lines, a mile or so to the rear and front respectively, were 300 feet higher. The slightly elevated outpost had been in American hands for some time and had been fortified in a rough circle with sandbagged bunkers connected by a communication trench, all surrounded by barbed wire interspersed with trip flares to signal enemy attempts to breach the perimeter. During the infrequent periods of combat, the Americans fought from the trenches. In between, they slept and ate in the bunkers. Eerie, like many other such American outposts, performed two purposes. First, it was used as a nighttime patrol base—a safe harbor from which to dispatch, support, or retrieve friendly patrols. Second, its possession by U.S. forces deprived the Chinese of the same sort of use.

On the night of March 21–22, 1952, the outpost was under the command of Lieutenant Omer Manley, a platoon leader, and his twenty-five men from Company K, 179th Infantry. Manley had telephone contact via wire with the U.S. lines and his company commander. Two American patrols were operating from Eerie that night. One, called the Raider Patrol, was trying to capture a Chinese prisoner for interrogation. The other was from K Company, a nine-man unit that was setting up an ambush. What happened that night was told by the survivors, both American and Chinese, to Major B. C. Mossman and Lieutenant Edgar Denton:

Bunker life in the 45th Division. *During the last phase of the war, the lines became largely static and elaborate defensive positions were common. This photo shows a fighting bunker in the U.S. 45th Division sector, one that was connected to other defensive positions by trenches. Note the hand grenades ready for use. Other bunkers were not intended for fighting, being used for sleeping, but placed near fighting positions.*

"Darkness came early on the night of 21 March. It stopped raining about 8 P.M. soon after the two patrols had established their ambush points, but the night remained dark, misty, and cold. Since the enemy had probed Outpost Eerie on the two previous nights, Lieutenant Manley considered some enemy activity probable."

In the meantime, Chinese units with similar missions just across from the American lines were being prepared. The next day, a wounded Chinese soldier was left on the battlefield and picked up by the Americans. Under interrogation, he told his story to a U.S. Army interpreter:

". . . On the night of 21 March, (he had) eaten the evening meal just before dark, as usual. He and the other men of his squad had then gone to sleep. Some time between 7 and 8 P.M., the squad leader awakened them and told them to prepare for a patrol. . . . After standing in the dark for a short while, each squad present reported its strength. There were three rifle squads, two machine-gun squads and one grenade-discharger squad, having a combined total of about sixty men according to the count.

"The Chinese patrol leader then delivered a pep talk, telling his men their mission was to capture some U.S. soldiers, and that they should go out and fight gallantly. When the talk was finished, the enemy soldiers moved out to emplace their supporting weapons and prepare to attack. The three rifle squads, moving in a column with one and a half yards between men, followed their leader over the . . . ridge toward the outpost position. A similar enemy force was moving along the opposite side of the ridge. Thirty minutes later the fight began."

The firing had come from the American Raider patrol that had spotted the much larger Chinese force. This patrol leader called Outpost Eerie, informed Lieutenant Manley of the approaching Chinese, and told him they were abandoning the attempt to pick up a Chinese prisoner. Manley then called his company commander, Captain Max Clark, saying:

" 'The raiders have made contact with a large group of Chinks on their front, left, and right, but did not stop

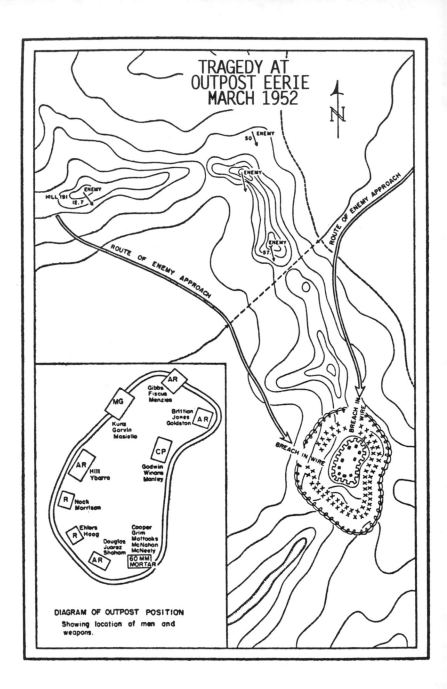

TRAGEDY AT
OUTPOST EERIE
MARCH 1952

N

SO ENEMY

ENEMY

HILL 191   ENEMY
12.7

ENEMY
57

ROUTE OF ENEMY APPROACH

ROUTE OF ENEMY APPROACH

BREACH IN WIRE

BREACH IN WIRE

AR
Gibbs
Fiscus
Menzies

MG
Kurz
Garvin
Masiello

Brittian
Jones
Goldston

AR

CP

AR
Hill
Ybarra

Godwin
Winans
Manley

R
Nock
Morrison

R
Ehlers
Hoog

Cooper
Grim
Mattocks
McMahon
McNeely

Douglas
Juarez
Shaham

AR

60 MM
MORTAR

DIAGRAM OF OUTPOST POSITION
Showing location of men and
weapons.

138

them.'. . . 'The patrol has broken contact and is withdrawing. . . . We're cocked and primed and ready for anything.'

"Lieutenant Manley remarked . . . 'I'd sure like to know where the hell they (the Raiders) are!'. . .

"Manley was uncertain whether the sounds at the wire were made by the friendly patrol, or by the Chinese. The attack came at 11:30 P.M. Two trip flares went off beyond the lowest barbed wire entanglement. . . .

"Lieutenant Manley, still in doubt about the identity of the men outside the wire, rushed over from the command post bunker, yelling not to fire.

" 'It's the Raider Patrol returning!' he shouted.

" 'Like hell it is!' answered Sergeant Calvin P. Jones. 'They're not talking English. It's the Chinese! Come on, let's get it on!'

"It was then that two enemy machineguns opened fire and began sweeping the outpost position."

K Company's mortars were fired in support of Manley's beleaguered outpost and the lieutenant reported on the fight and made corrections over the radio.

". . .'They are giving us a hell of a battle out here, but we're OK so far. . . . Bring the mortars in closer. . . . That's too close! . . . Move 'em out a little. . . . Now, leave them right where they are.'

"As far as anyone in the perimeter could determine, the Chinese were trying to break through the barbed wire at only two places, the attacks coming from the north and the northeast. For another three quarters of an hour the defenders held off both attacks without further casualties [one American dead thus far] . . . Lieutenant Manley called the company's command post and asked the artillery forward observer to fire artillery concentration No.

304, which was plotted . . . on the ridgefinger. Harassing artillery fire had been falling on this area throughout the evening—a few shells at intervals of about twenty minutes.

"A little later, about half an hour after midnight, when Captain Clark telephoned to the outpost to ask how things were going, Private Leroy Winans replied, 'Everything's OK, sir, they're not through the wire yet.'

"Meanwhile, both enemy assault groups steadily pressed their attempts to blow gaps in the circle of protective wire. At least one of the groups was using bangalore torpedoes.

"Mortar and artillery illuminating flares contributed greatly to the defense, but whenever the illumination failed, the flash of the defenders' weapons betrayed their positions to the enemy. When the supply of mortar illumination shells was exhausted, a 155-mm battery fired an illumination mission. Most of these shells, however, burst too close to the ground to furnish effective light. Despite all efforts to adjust the height of burst, it was not corrected in time to help.

"Effective illuminating fire ceased before 1 A.M., 22 March. About this time Private Robert L. Fiscus, an automatic rifleman in the bunker to the immediate right of the light machine gun, was wounded. Corporal Herman Godwin had been assisting at the machine gun, crawled to his right through the communication trench and found Fiscus lying in the trench outside of the bunker. Carrying the wounded man inside, Godwin dressed the wound. . . .

"Private Hugh Menzies, Jr., was the next man wounded. As Godwin came out of the bunker after dressing Fiscus's wound, he saw Menzies get hit by grenade fragments. Godwin pulled him into the bunker with Fiscus and administered first aid.

"By 1 A.M., the enemy had breached the wire in two places. Lieutenant Manley encouraged his men, calling out to them, 'Get up and fight or we'll be wiped out! This isn't any movie!'

"Private Elbert Goldston was the next man wounded. As the Chinese soldiers came through the breaks in the wire and up the hill toward the outpost, he was hit in both legs by burp gun fire, and in the arm and head by shell fragments. Of the nine men occupying the three bunkers facing the enemy attack, four were now out of action, two were dead. . . .

"Several minutes had elapsed since the enemy broke through the wire and started crawling up toward the outpost defenses. Godwin now discovered that there were no grenades left in the center bunker. He grabbed his rifle and began firing into the advancing Chinese from a position in the communication trench. The enemy troops were very near the top. Godwin fired until his ammunition was gone, threw his rifle at the nearest Chinese and saw the butt hit him in the face, knocking him down the hill. He then ducked into the bunker to look after the two wounded men and as he did so, noticed Corporal Carl F. Brittian throwing BAR magazines at the approaching Chinese. Brittian was killed very soon afterward. . . .

"Corporal Godwin . . . had the feeling that he must be the only able-bodied man left. Stepping out of the bunker for a look, he spotted a Chinese soldier coming along the trench toward him. He stepped back against the bunker, waited until the Chinese was within point-blank range, and shot him in the head with a caliber .45 pistol. Knowing the report would attract attention, Godwin jumped back against the side of the trench. An enemy soldier standing on the edge of the trench fired a burst from his burp gun, but then moved on without determining whether he had hit Godwin. With nothing but a dent in the lip of his helmet,

Godwin went back into the bunker. Moments later an enemy soldier threw a concussion grenade through the entrance opposite the one by which Godwin had just entered . . . the explosion knocked Godwin unconscious and bent the metal cover of a small Bible he carried in his left breast pocket. . . .

"Shortly after the Chinese broke through the wire, Private Winans, who by this time was the only man left at the command post bunker, called Captain Clark.

" 'They're coming through the wire and it looks like a thousand!' Winans said. 'It looks like we're going to have to surrender!'

" 'No; don't surrender!' the company commander replied. 'Get Lieutenant Manley.' This happened at about the same time the Chinese were overrunning the bunker on the opposite side of the hill where Lieutenant Manley had been.

"Right after this an enemy shell—probably one from a 57-mm recoilless rifle—made a direct hit on the command post bunker. It killed Winans and cut all telephone lines to Company K. There was no more communication with Outpost Eerie.

"Back at the company's observation post, Captain Clark told his artillery liaison officer, Lieutenant Anthony Cotroneo, to shift his artillery from two concentrations being fired at the time and to place it squarely on Outpost Eerie itself. In a few minutes, 105-mm proximity-fuse shells began bursting over the position. [These shells explode in the air, showering the ground below with lethal fragments.] There followed the sound of a horn blown three times, and within a few minutes enemy activity stopped. The artillery shells fell, and the enemy's recall signal sounded before the Chinese troops had covered the entire outpost area. . . . The Chinese withdrew, assembling near the break in the wire they had made at the northwest part of the perimeter. They left two of their dead in the position.

"At 1:30 A.M., the regimental commander, Colonel Frederick A. Daugherty, ordered Captain Clark to move the rest of Company K up to the relief of the outpost. . . . Thirty-five minutes later, after a platoon from Company A took over its position on the main line of resistance, Company K moved out.

"Company K reached Eerie at 4 A.M. . . . Once on top, the men searched the area for casualties, and evacuated them as they were located. . . .

"Of the twenty-six men who had defended Outpost Eerie, eight were dead, four wounded and two were missing in action. With one exception, all men killed had suffered head and chest wounds—the parts of their bodies exposed above the firing positions in the communication trench. . . . It was Captain Clark's opinion that the artillery fire which fell on the outpost after the Chinese had entered it had prevented further casualties. He felt the [artillery] air-bursts forced the Chinese to withdraw before they were able to cover the entire outpost area in a thorough search. . . .

"The men found only two enemy dead within the barbed wire surrounding the outpost, but found twenty-nine other bodies to the north and northwest along the enemy's route of withdrawal. . . ."

During this talk-fight phase, the Communists had perceived advantages that the Allies tried to offset. The assumption on the U.N. side was that their adversaries could keep up this kind of war indefinitely. After all, there seemed to be no regard for human life in either the Chinese or the North Korean armies, and the enemy soldiers, being of peasant stock, were believed to be inured to the hardships of cold, hunger, and danger. Additionally, Communist societies were thought to be highly disciplined, so that there would be little if any public problem about having an unlucky part of a nation's youth endure a long and possibly permanent separation from their families. In short, the Allies believed the Communists could handle misery longer and had decided to win the war by merely outlasting the U.N.

To compensate, the American leadership did everything it could to make troop life in Korea as comfortable and endurable as possible. The most popular program was the rotation system. Depending on the availability of replacements, a frontline American soldier would be due to return to the United States after he had served eleven months during 1952. This tour length varied throughout the war. At one point, fighters had only to endure six months in combat. Rear-area troops had to remain in Korea for a longer period. Both categories, frontline and rear-echelon troops, got a much-sought-after break, a five-day rest and recreation visit to Japan, sometime during their Korean tour of duty. Another attempt to make life bearable revolved around the food Americans ate. Major Lawrence Dobson of the Quartermaster Corps came home from Korea with some observations:

"As you have heard, troops in Korea are fed two hot meals a day whenever it is tactically possible. It is desirable, of course, to have three hot meals, but we say a minimum of two: normally, breakfast and supper. Noon meals are an operational ration . . . the troops and the leaders appreciate the benefit of kitchen-prepared meals. It's a terrific morale builder among the forward elements. . . .

"The C ration is the most acceptable (field) ration we have in use in Korea. Everyone likes it. The relative acceptance ratings of the meat items are: 1) beans and frankfurters; (2) beans with pork; (3) meat and beans; (4) ham and lima beans; (5) spaghetti and meat; (6) hamburger and gravy; (7) pork sausage patties with gravy; (8) meat and noodles; (9) chicken and vegetables; (10) beef stew; (11) corned-beef hash.

"This ration is a combat ration, and one of its characteristics is its capability of being consumed hot or cold. The reaction of the men was that the only items acceptable cold were the three bean items. The principal complaints were against the meat-and-spaghetti and the meat-and-

C ration lunch break. *Privates Donald A. Johnson and Joseph MacNamara of the 15th Infantry enjoy some noontime nourishment, February 1953. MacNamara's cigar was not included in the Quartermaster-developed rations, but small packs of cigarettes were.*

noodle combinations. Both items were too dry, and when heated they would burn. The hamburgers and the sausage patties had too much fat and too much gravy. It is difficult to determine the acceptance of the chicken and vegetables. In the C-4 and the C-6 [previous Army combat rations] we had a chicken and vegetables combination. The men disliked it. We had previously received reports on this, and in the C-7 we have a product of the same name but from a different formula. The men interviewed who have eaten the C-7 have reported that the acceptance on the chicken-and-vegetables was high. It is a very good product. . . .

"When I asked, 'What do you think of the individual combat ration?' the first thing said was, 'Where is the spoon in the C-6?' And the next thing: 'The C-7 is a lot better ration; it has a spoon.'

"As I mentioned before, the men carry nothing. Mess kits are kept in kitchen trucks. Soldiers are stripped down—no packs—just the clothes they wear. We also used to think a man would never lose his eating utensils. That is not so. They lose them, and unit commanders have them resupplied as fast as they are needed. In many cases forks and spoons are kept in the kitchen. At first the C ration came without spoons, and we got reports of men eating beans with their fingers. One Marine colonel cut his finger in trying to make a spoon from the lid of a can. I would say—and I am stating the opinion of everyone interviewed—that plastic spoons are a must in the operational rations.

"In the past we included a can opener in each accessory packet. Every soldier I saw had a can opener in his pocket or on his dogtag chain. He was afraid he would not have a can opener when he wanted to eat. If he had a can opener and got hold of another, he saved it. My prize example is a colonel who had one can opener on his dogtag chain and nine in his pack. So my recommendation is that the can openers be reduced to two or three per case and that they no longer be packed in the accessory pack, but be placed on top."

Efforts were also made to provide American troops with a chance to keep clean. Lieutenant Colonel Kenneth O. Schellberg, quartermaster of the 7th Infantry Division, recalls:

"We learned that the quartermaster's shower and clothing exchange was a great economy in spite of the additional equipment necessary to allow the men to bathe and to launder their clothing. . . .

"When the clothing exchange began, we collected all the duffel bags and limited each soldier to the clothing on his back plus a change of under clothing and socks. . . . Thus the total number of uniforms per man dropped from three sets to one and a half. . . .

"There were many advantages to the clothing exchange system. It cut down the weight the soldier had to carry; it also eliminated duffel bags and the thirty-man detail in each regiment to guard and handle them. This increased our mobility. The cleaner clothing improved the hygiene of the troops, and the automatic exchange of clothing eliminated all requisitions below division. Exchange made possible early repair of shirts and trousers before they became unsalvageable. . . .

"We learned that in combat there is no need to publish a shower schedule because company commanders preferred to send men to showers whenever the tactical situation permitted. From experience we learned that the shower units should not be moved farther forward than regiment. . . .

"The shower and clothing exchange was a great morale builder for the men. After an attack in which a regiment was unable to release men to get showers, we would augment its bathing facilities and see that every man could bathe and change within four days. Normally, however, the men had a shower once a week.

"Company commanders watched their men for signs of excessive fatigue and sent them to the showers when a relief seemed necessary. Often a shower and a hot meal at regiment were enough to restore a soldier's efficiency. If the fatigue were dangerous, the soldier could be sent to the regimental rest camp for a day or two of sleep, hot meals, and regular baths. This was an excellent way to prevent combat fatigue."

As the truce talks droned on and the war of outposts and patrols continued, another, more mobile war was in progress behind Communist lines. When the winter snows of early 1952 melted, there was every indication this American-directed guerrilla campaign would become even more intense. On April 11 the controlling headquarters for the effort, the 8240 Army Unit, published "Guerrilla Operations Outline, 1952." The document contained some surprising directives:

"1. *General.* The increased activities of the guerrilla units with the advent of spring weather has been noted favorably by this and higher headquarters. The severe Korean winter understandably curtailed many of our operations during January, February and early March. We are now entering the most favorable time of the year for launching guerrilla and partisan projects. We are able to strike the enemy an even more telling blow this year than we did in 1951. The experience and training gained in our operations during 1951 will enable guerrilla commanders to take seasoned men into combat this year. Communications have improved and our supply levels are higher by far than they were at the beginning of the 1951 operational season. . . .

"8. *Privateering*. Individual privateers will be encouraged to engage the enemy for the purpose of either seizing enemy small craft or destroying them. The cargo should be given to the privateer to encourage further attacks on shipping. Captured vessels can be repaired with our facilities in order to enable the privateer to better attack additional targets. . . .

"10. *Chinese Guerrillas*. Efforts will be made to develop Chinese guerrillas from deserters from the CCF [Chinese Communist Forces]. Reports reaching this headquarters indicate that limited numbers of former Nationalists are deserting the CCF and forming guerrilla bands. These will be supported and encouraged to enlarge their guerrilla tactics. The locations, strengths and activities of Chinese guerrillas will be reported as obtained in order that action can be taken to establish liaison with them.

"11. *North Korean Currency*. Due to the large requirements for North Korean Currency and the limited sources available, commanders will encourage bank robberies and other suitable means of procuring this currency. . . .

"19. *Assassinations*. Primary assassination targets are Korean Communist leaders. Communist or North Korea Labor Party leaders who will not render partisan assistance to our forces will be assassinated. If succeeding Communist leaders are assassinated, the ambitions of minor leaders will be dampened. This has already been demonstrated by our efforts in some sectors. Terrorist tactics of focusing attention on the high mortality rate of enemy leaders are to be encouraged. Only selected Soviets should be assassinated. They should be of sufficient rank or possess sufficient technical knowledge that the gain will compensate for the resultant countermeasures that will be taken by the enemy. Soviets should be assassinated in areas that abound with pro-Communists. This creates suspicion and doubt between the Soviets and their satellite Korean followers. Korean Communist leaders should be assassinated wherever found."

There was also an armed conflict going on in the U.N. rear. This conflict grew to dominate the negotiations and thus control whether the war would stop or continue. Simply put, this battle in the U.N. rear was an intensely ideological war over individual rights. It emerged shortly after the truce talks resumed in November 1951, when the U.N. Command became aware of the fact that some of the 132,000 "Communist" prisoners it held wished to live under a different form of gov-

Going on a brief visit home. North Korean partisans on an offshore island loading a junk in preparation for a raid on the mainland, 1952.

ernment in the postwar world than the type that had sent them to war. However, there seemed to be little initial American concern about this situation. The primary thought on the part of the U.N. negotiators was the anticipated return of the 11,559 U.N. prisoners held by the Communists. By April 1952 the issue, increasingly dubbed the "repatriation question," gradually began to overshadow all other truce talk agenda items.

In some respects, the violent manifestation of the repatriation question was a product of the lack of manpower the Americans allocated to watch over the prisoners they had collected. Generally, a 20 to 1 ratio of prisoners to guards is recommended for prisoner of war camps. At first, the U.S. only managed a ridiculous 188 to 1 ratio. By adding ROK Army personnel to assist in caring for and watching over the prisoners, the ratio was reduced to 33 to 1, still short of the personnel resources required to adequately maintain control. The situation was further alleviated by assigning some of the willing and capable prisoners to look after the needs of others. Thus, by the end of 1951, a prisoner hierarchy existed. The Americans relied on this internal, wholly prisoner organization to keep order, maintain prison camp sanitation, see that there was a fair distribution of food and clothing, and to report on conditions. In truth, the Americans had never established effective management over their captives. One of the ROK Army officers, Lieutenant Kim Sun Ho, assigned to assist the U.S. forces, described an incident that revealed much about the lack of American control. In Lieutenant Kim's view and in the view of some of the prisoners who were South Koreans, unfortunate souls who had been pressed into the North Korean Army and subsequently captured by the U.N., Americans were "just indifferent." Lieutenant Kim:

. . . **April 28, 1952.** General Mark W. Clark appointed to replace General Ridgway, who is designated to take General Eisenhower's position as N.A.T.O. commander . . . **May 7, 1952.** Communist prisoners temporarily seize U.S. Brigadier General Francis T. Dodd as hostage.

"One day a North Korean prisoner was somewhat seriously beaten up by the South Korean prisoner police [pris-
oners who had been delegated to keep order in the prison
compounds, generally known by the term "hanchoes"].
This immediately attracted the attention of the camp authorities [the Americans]. The authorities did not try to find
out the reason why the man should be treated like that,
instead, they transferred the chief of police [head of the
prisoner guards] out of the compound. This caused a big
sensation among the South Korean hanchoes, because the
police chief was a great [i.e., an important and powerful]
man. Without him the morale of the rest would certainly
become low. One of the South Korean hanchoes remarked:
'I do not know what the American people are fighting for.
We should cooperate with each other to pick out the Communists in the compounds, but the camp authority doesn't
even help us.' As a matter of fact, the North Korean who
was beaten up was a North Korean cultural officer who was
seen to be instigating the rest of the prisoners."

In the absence of American interest, the anti-Communists
organized their own means to change their official "Communist" status. Anti-Communist sentiment was not confined to the
South Koreans who happened to be in the Communist ranks
when captured. There were also some Chinese who sought the
same change. Wang Shun-ching, a former Nationalist Chinese
officer who had been drafted into Communist ranks, was among
the first of the Chinese prisoners taken by U.N. forces. When he
arrived at an American-run prison compound near Pusan, he
was confronted by another Chinese captive, Wang Fu-tien, who
was already at work converting newcomers to the anti-
Communist cause:

"We have suffered much under the cruel control of the
Communists and now we have a chance to get out of their

control, so we must make up our mind that we are never going back to Red China and suffer more from the Communists."

Ten of the first sixty Chinese prisoners joined Wang Fu-tien and helped him enlist more recruits among the steadily rising numbers of captives. Communists also organized and competed for the newly arrived prisoners of war. Thus, an intensely political enlistment effort was going on under the noses of the American prison authorities. In September 1951 words were replaced with violence. Fifteen prisoners were murdered by a "court" within a prison compound and rioting broke out at the site, Koje-do, an island off the southern coast of the Peninsula. By the end of the year, U.S. combat troops had to be dispatched to keep the peace between the Communist and anti-Communist factions. For the Communist negotiators in the truce talks, the ugly situation threatened to be a major source of embarrassment for the worldwide Marxist movement. During his October 24, 1952, talk, Secretary of State Acheson recounted how the prisoner issue developed:

"Let us talk for a moment about the background of the prisoner question. From the very beginning, the United Nations Command has followed the provisions of the Geneva Convention of 1949, and it has particularly done so by promptly sending lists of prisoners to the International Committee of the Red Cross which, in turn, has sent these lists to the other side. Vast numbers of prisoners have been captured by the United Nations side. One hundred and seventy thousand odd names were sent in. Subsequently, it was discovered that during the period of the wholesale surrenders by the North Korean Army and the

... **October 8, 1952.** U.N. calls indefinite recess in truce talks after Communists launch major offensive. . . . .

mass movement of refugees from the North, 37,000 odd
people were sent into these prisoner of war camps who
were not prisoners at all. These were civilian people and
they were reclassified—some 37,000 odd people—and
they were freed. The International Committee of the Red
Cross was informed of these people by name. Subsequently, we gave a revised list to the Communists containing 132,000 names. Investigation of these revealed that
11,000 were Republic of Korea citizens. . . . and they too
are being released. [This may be a disingenuous statement
by the Secretary. Some of the 37,000 may have been
"civilians," but it is likely the bulk were both North and
South Koreans who had been forcibly pressed into the
North Korean Army and were able to convince American
authorities of their actual status and desire not to be repatriated to North Korea.] The United Nations Command,
therefore, has in custody, as prisoners of war, about
121,000 persons.

"As compared with what I have just reported as to
United Nations observance of the Geneva Convention, the
Communist practice has been not to inform the International Committee of the Red Cross or the United Nations
Command, through any channel, of the names and numbers of prisoners of war, as required by law. When they
finally agreed to list the prisoners of war, they listed
11,500, including all Koreans and all United Nations Command prisoners. This was disappointing because, only
months before, on April 8, 1951—and before that, on
February 9, 1951—the Communists had announced over
the radio that, in the first nine months of hostilities, they
had captured 65,000 persons. They were very proud of it
and they announced it over the radio twice—65,000 prisoners in the first nine months of hostilities. But when they
were asked about the difference between 65,000 and
11,500, they had a most interesting explanation. They said

that the difference was accounted for by people who had been "re-educated" at the front—so quickly that it was impossible to get their names. Most of these people had almost instantaneously been re-educated—and had done what? What do you suppose these re-educatees had done so quickly that one could not get their names? You have guessed it, I am sure: they joined the North Korean Army. And that was the difference between 65,000 and 11,500.

"In the treatment of prisoners of war, the United Nations Command has not only sent the lists, but it has admitted the International Committee of the Red Cross to its prisoner of war camps; it has given the Committee every facility to investigate every camp; and, on every occasion on which it has been criticized by the International Committee for any conduct, it has promptly met that criticism and changed what was going on in the camp.

"Communist practice, as I have said, has been that they have not given lists of names. They have failed to appoint a protecting power or a benevolent organization such as the Red Cross. They rejected the efforts of the International Committee of the Red Cross to get into the Communist prisoner of war camps. They have refused to exchange relief packages and, until very recently, they have refused to exchange mail—and now that it is allowed, only on a most limited scale. They have refused to report on the health of prisoners of war and they refuse to exchange the seriously sick and wounded as is required by the Geneva Convention. They have failed to give the accurate locations of the prisoner of war camps and have failed to mark them properly, and they have situated their camps in places of danger near legitimate military targets, a defiance of the Geneva Convention.

"We now come to the origin of this repatriation question. As increasing numbers of prisoners came into United Nations hands, it began to be found out that more and

more of these prisoners believed that, if they were returned to Communist hands, they would be executed or
imprisoned or treated brutally in some way. They therefore took the position that they would not be exchanged
and that, if an attempt was made to exchange them, they
would resist by force. It was quite unthinkable to the
United Nations Command that it should use force to drive
into the hands of the Communists people that would be
resisting that effort by force. That was the attitude taken by
the United Nations Command. It was the attitude taken by
all other Governments whose troops were in Korea and
who would be required to carry out this forcible return if it
were instituted. So far as I know there has been no member
of the United Nations outside the Communist group that
has ever suggested that it was right, proper, legal or necessary to return these prisoners by force.

"Even our knowledge that many of the prisoners had
this attitude did not give us the slightest idea of the magni-
tude of the problem until the interrogation period came
along in April 1952. At that time, when we saw the numbers who held these views and the violence with which
they held them, it became clear that it would not only be
highly immoral and illegal to force these prisoners to
return, but that it would also require a military operation
of no inconsiderable proportions to do it. . . .

"Now let me talk for a moment about the so-called
screening of prisoners which really means the interrogat-
ing of the prisoners to find out whether or not they would
resist violently a return to the Communist side . . . how did
that come about? It came about in this way: In April 1952
when we were arguing with the Communists as to this
principle, they said: 'Well, how many people are involved
in this? Let us find out whether this is a serious question
before we just argue about it on principle. How many of
these prisoners do you say would violently resist going

back?' And we said: "The only way we can find out is to ask them. We don't know any other way of finding out. And we think it would be very helpful and very much to your interests on the Communist side if you put out a proclamation of amnesty so that we could tell anybody who was worried about himself that you are ready to pardon him.' The Communists said: 'That is a good idea; we will do that.' And so they put out a proclamation of amnesty for any prisoner of war who would return—for the very purpose of affecting, if they could, the decisions of the prisoners during this period of interrogation. Therefore, when they say that this is all wrong and wicked and illegal, what you have to know is that they themselves agreed to it.

"We tried to be as careful and as fair in the screening as we possibly could. In order to achieve that, the interrogation of the Chinese prisoners of war was done exclusively by United States military personnel; there were no [Nationalist] Chinese personnel used in that operation. In the case of the Koreans, it was very largely United States military personnel, but in some cases others assisted. . . .

"The original screening of prisoners of war in April applied only to those who were in camps where interrogation was permitted. In some of the camps, the Communist leaders of the prisoners refused to permit any interrogation, and such interrogation was not possible until later. Thus, the first results were that 70,000 would be available for repatriation. In most camps where we could not carry on an interrogation, we had to estimate, and that was done on the basis that most of these prisoners would want to return. Therefore, we reported that there were 70,000 who would be available for repatriation.

"Even in the camps where the Communist leaders were in complete control and where no interrogation was permitted, a thousand prisoners escaped at the earliest possible moment to get away from these leaders, and a considerable number who attempted to escape were murdered by their own fellow Communist prisoners of war.

"Subsequently, the United Nations Command completed the interviewing of all those who had not been screened previously, and reported that 83,000 wished to be repatriated. This number was made up of 76,600 Korean and 6,400 Chinese. They were the ones who said they would not violently resist repatriation.

"But let me say here, as we have said over and over again, that the United Nations is willing to have all this screening redone by any impartial party in the world. We have made that offer over and over again. The Command has done the best it can, but it does not set itself up as final and absolute, and if any other group of people acceptable to all and whose word would be taken could do that screening, then let them do it by all means."

The day after Secretary Acheson explained the reasons for the truce talk impasse over the prisoner issue, October 24, 1952, a controversial recommendation from the U.S. Defense Department landed on President Truman's desk. It advocated the authorization of money and matériel to greatly expand South Korea's Army, raising its strength to almost a half million men. The increase would give this force some twelve divisions. This recommendation represented a sharp change of course. While a number of programs had been instituted to improve ROK Army leadership, the previous U.S. military position had been that the South Korean ground organization should remain at a strength of ten divisions. The rationale, usually voiced by General Ridgway, had been that the existing quality of leadership within the force did not argue for more mediocre officers, but a smaller number of qualified leaders. However, Ridgway had been replaced in the spring of 1952 by General Mark W. Clark, and the new commander not only reinforced Ridgway's ROK Army leadership programs, he vigorously added new capabilities and encouraged his superiors to expand this young force. Major Robert K. Sawyer recounted the changes in South Korea's ground arm:

"During late 1951 and early 1952 KMAG [the American-staffed Korean Military Advisory Group] began to stimulate the growth of the existing educational facilities and to establish new ones. Schools that had been closed by the North Korean invasion were reopened. By the first of October 1951, the ROKA [ROK Army] schools were operating with a capacity of over 10,000 students at a time. . . .

"To provide additional training for future company officers, the courses at the officer candidate schools were lengthened from eighteen to twenty-four weeks during the winter of 1951, and the Korean Military Academy was re-established at a new location at Chinhae. On January 1, 1952, a full four-year course patterned after West Point was initiated and the first class of two hundred cadets began their instruction. For field grade officers [major to colonel], the Command and General Staff School was reopened.

"To supplement the ROK Army school system, the [U.S.] Department of the Army had approved a KMAG request for 250 ROK officers to attend U.S. service schools in late 1951. A hundred and fifty officers were enrolled at the Infantry School at Benning, and the other hundred participated in the course at the Artillery School at Fort Sill. . . .

"In addition to raising officer standards, KMAG also sought to bolster the morale and combat capabilities of the troops at the front. . . . members of the KMAG staff helped supervise the establishment of four training camps, one in each corps area, to retrain the ROK Army. Since many individuals and units had been forced by the exigencies of battle to enter combat with very little training, the respite on the battlefield provided a chance for the ROK divisions to fill in some of the gaps in their military education. As each division came back from the front and went into corps reserve, it was sent to a field training center for nine weeks of basic training. Refresher instruction in weapons and tactics began with the individual and worked up to squad, platoon, and company level. At the end of the course, a battalion problem was presented and worked out. . . . by late 1952, all of the ten original ROK divisions had received at least five weeks of refresher training. . . .

"The lack of adequate integral artillery in the ROK division had been recognized early in the war, for the ROK Army only had one 105-mm howitzer battalion assigned to a division while the American counterpart had three 105-mm and one 155-mm howitzer battalions as a normal complement. Moreover, the U.S. division also had a tank battalion and heavy mortar companies to call upon for additional fire support. As long as the war had been in a mobile phase, the Far East Command and the Eighth Army staffs had frowned upon increasing the ROK artillery. They had felt that the rugged terrain, the difficulty of ammunition resupply, the lack of trained ROK artillery-men, and the shortage of artillery pieces all argued against expansion.

"Time and the stalemate at the front overcame these objections. In September 1951 General Ridgway authorized four 155-mm howitzer battalions to be activated before the end of the year. As each was activated it was attached to a U.S. corps and trained for eight weeks. Three headquarters batteries and six 105-mm howitzer battalions were authorized in November 1951 and began training two months later. The continued lull on the battlefield and the availability of more artillery pieces and of trained ROKA artillery officers as they returned from the U.S. Artillery

School, provided added incentives for further increases. Ridgway set up a program that eventually would produce sufficient 105-mm and 155-mm battalions to give each of the ten ROK divisions a full complement of three 105-mm and one 155-mm howitzer artillery battalions. . . .

"To strengthen the ROK fire power, KMAG began training armored troops at the [ROK] Infantry School in April 1951. The object was to provide one tank company for each ROK division . . . in October, the first two companies were activated and trained. . . . It was not until the spring of 1952 that M-24 light tanks arrived from the United States and that additional tank companies could be prepared for operations."

As the ROK Army improved its leadership, training, and equipment, fighting had been relatively light, but all that changed on October 6, 1952, when the Communists staged their largest offensive of the year. The truce talks were suspended and it appeared the war, on a full-blown scale, would resume. The Chinese, doubtlessly with their experience of overawing the South Koreans, chose to place the heaviest weight of their attack on a sector of the front defended by the ROK 9th Division, a unit commanded by Major General Kim Jong Oh. General Kim's troops were defending a hill mass dubbed by the Americans as White Horse Hill. A U.S. Army historian and veteran of World War II, Dr. Walter G. Hermes, studied this action:

". . . two battalions of the 340th Regiment, 114th Division, Chinese Communist Forces 38th Army, moved up to the northwest end of the White Horse Hill complex. After heavy artillery and mortar fire placed on the ROK 9th Division positions on the heights, the Chinese tried three times to penetrate the ROK defenses. Each time they were hurled back by troops of the ROK 30th Regiment, suffering an estimated 1,500 casualties the first night as against only 300 for the defenders. Notwithstanding the heavy losses, the Chinese committed the remnants of the original two battalions and reinforced them with two fresh battalions from the same division the following day. Cutting off a ROK company outpost, the Chinese pressed on and forced the elements of the 30th Regiment to withdraw from the crest. Less than two hours after the loss of the peak, two battalions of the ROK 28th Regiment mounted a night attack that swept the enemy out of the old ROK positions. Again the enemy losses were heavy and a Chinese prisoner later related that many of the companies committed to the attack were reduced to less than twenty men after the second day of the fighting. . . .

"Nothing daunted, the Chinese committed another battalion to the attack the following day. General Kim . . . moved two battalions of his 29th Regiment over to . . . help the 28th Regiment. Throughout the day the battle seesawed as first one side controlled the peak, then the other. Early on October 10, the 29th Regiment reported that it was in possession of the crest. . . .

"On October 12 there was a break in the bitter struggle. The 30th ROK Regiment passed through the dug-in 29th Regiment and counterattacked. In the morning the 28th Regiment moved up through the 30th and pressed the assault. Leapfrogging the battalions of the leading regiment and substituting attack regiments from time to time, the ROK 9th Division began to inflict extremely large casualties on the enemy. By October 15, the battle for White Horse was over.

"Although the Chinese had used a force estimated at 15,000 infantry and 8,000 supporting troops during the ten-day contest, they had failed to budge the ROK 9th Division. Despite ROK losses of over 3,500 soldiers during the nine ROK and twenty-eight Communist attacks, the 9th Division and its supporting troops had exacted a heavy toll from the Chinese 38th Army. Seven of the 38th Army's nine regiments had been committed to the White Horse and Hill 281 battles and taken close to 10,000 casualties."

Two weeks later, President Truman approved the Defense Department's recommendation. The United States would support a large-scale and expensive program to expand the ROK Army. In Washington some hoped that one day this expanding army would replace the American force manning the trenches and bunkers in an apparently endless war.

A TRUCE OF SORTS

November 1952–July 1953

THE POLICY CHANGE on U.S. support of the ROK Army attracted considerable favorable public commentary in America, but it was only one of a number of shifts in Washington's management of the war in the last months of 1952 and the early weeks of 1953. Dwight D. Eisenhower had been elected President in November, and many Americans believed the former general would find a way to either win or end what many were coming to believe as pointless, unending bloodletting in Korea. Before his inauguration, Eisenhower kept a campaign promise and visited the front. In his February 1953 State of the Union message, he revised the Truman policy of maintaining a U.S. Navy patrol between Taiwan and mainland China. Some believed this action would cause the Communists to shift some

February 22, 1953. General Clark proposes exchange of sick and wounded prisoners . . . .

military forces from Korea in order to defend the mainland's beaches from the threat of Chiang Kai-shek's large, island-based army. But the most immediate and promising change Americans welcomed was the addition of more ROK troops at the front, an idea the incoming Republicans referred to as "Asian wars fought by Asians." With the truce talks in recess since October, many in the U.S. were warmly embracing this notion as the most likely way out of Korea for American soldiers. A week after the new President's speech, General James Van Fleet, home from being replaced by Lieutenant General Maxwell Taylor as the Eighth Army commander, was closely questioned by members of the House Armed Services Committee of the Congress on the subject of just how many troops South Korea could produce:

CONGRESSMAN OVERTON BROOKS: . . . what recommendations do you have to make in reference to the additional use of the ROK troops?

VAN FLEET: First, Mr. Brooks, let me say that the ROK individual is a very fine fighting man. The Korean is a hardy individual. He is accustomed to getting along with very little in the way of food or clothing or general care. He is a very intelligent person, whether he has an education or not. He learns fast. You tell him once and he has it, or show him once and he has it. He is obedient, used to being bossed; endures hardship and suffering. And he is courageous. In battle he will do as he is told and keeps advancing, even after he is wounded, to close with the enemy.

Now he is as fine a type of fighting man as you could possibly want. In other words, we have no corner in America on aptitude for military bravery This oriental has all those splendid qualities.

He is, of course, a much cheaper man to maintain than an American boy, and he is on the spot. He doesn't have to be transported. His pay is 3,000 won a month, which is equivalent today to about ten cents a month. There are no allowances. There is no insurance, when he is gone, he is gone—left right there. That is the end of him.

So he is many, many times cheaper. And he is a superb soldier. Korea has quite a little bit of manpower still available. The Republic of Korea today is some 20 million people. Every one of them is willing to fight for freedom, including their women. The most magnificent thing about that nation is the fact that the women of the country tell their men they must fight for their home and freedom or give them the rifles and they will fight. In other words, they are magnificent home support to the fighting front.

The boy himself has seen some terrible calamity in his family where the Communists have killed or kidnapped or tortured some of them. He knows why he is fighting. And all the leaders of that country, from their great President, Syngman Rhee, on down through the chain of command, commands them to fight.

So you have a great spirit there to fight communism that backs up that manpower.

Now the manpower is available. There are only two things that nation has—manpower and a willingness to fight to victory. The people haven't anything else in the way of resources. So all that it takes to fight in the way of matériel must be supplied. It is a destroyed country, that has been fought over, down and back, and down and back again, four times. Their capital city of Seoul changed hands. It is a destroyed country.

BROOKS: Well, as I understand you to say—

VAN FLEET: Except their morale, which still lives on.

BROOKS: We could use more ROKs. They are available; that is correct, isn't it? Would you recommend that?

VAN FLEET: Yes, sir; I have advocated that always.

CONGRESSMAN CARL DURHAM: I understood you to mean in

your statement that they could be increased by ten more divisions, the ROK troops.

VAN FLEET: That is when we originally had ten of their divisions. We have gone from ten to fourteen in the last few months.

CONGRESSMAN JAMES E. VAN ZANDT: General, what is the potential from the standpoint of divisions for the Korean manpower?

VAN FLEET: They could go up to twenty divisions very readily, and support that number, with heavy casualties.

VAN ZANDT: With heavy casualties?

VAN FLEET: Yes, in active fighting.

VAN ZANDT: A moment ago you said that the Chinese represented four-fifths of the opposition on the front. That left the North Koreans representing one-fifth. Are the North Koreans having any difficulty replacing their casualties?

VAN FLEET: The North Koreans reached the bottom of their manpower a year ago. We do not find any people that have been brought into the [North] Korean Army in the last twelve, eighteen months; except a few who have been hiding out and they finally caught up with them.

VAN ZANDT: Now, who is supplying the North Korean divisions with their matériel of war?

VAN FLEET: Russia.

The character of the war was changing and a number of factors now favored the United Nations side. Although Communist soldiers had numbered about one million for some time as opposed to about 640,000 under the U.N. banner, the Chinese and North Korean attackers could not seem to make any progress. American airpower and firepower were apparently enough to offset the inferior numbers. Then, too, since the ROK Army was expanding rapidly, the American public's fatigue with the war might become less of a concern because the U.S. role was being diminished with each passing day. Less than six months before, in the summer of 1952, the U.S. contingent amounted to 39 percent of U.N. combat manpower, with the ROK share at 55 percent. Other Allied nations supplied only 6 percent, with the British Commonwealth force being the largest, about 20,000 troops. Now, in early 1953, the U.S. share had dropped to 32 percent and the ROK proportion had topped 63 percent, a number that was steadily climbing. When these figures and facts were coupled with the new Eisenhower administration's evident willingness to make bolder moves, momentum seemed to be with the U.N. side.

In Washington, hopes soared during March. When the long-time Soviet leader Joseph Stalin died on March 5, his successor, Georgi Malenkov, spoke of "peaceful coexistence" with the West. And, on the 28th, the Chinese and North Korean governments agreed with an American proposal to exchange sick and wounded prisoners. Liaison officers from both sides quickly worked out the details and 6,670 Chinese and North Koreans were handed over to the Communists. The U.N. regained 684 of its own troops who were serious medical cases while in Communist captivity.

However, on April 9, American optimism waned with the pronouncement of the chief Communist military negotiator, North Korean Lieutenant General Nam Il. Asked about a Communist Chinese statement that seemed to offer a quick settlement of the repatriation issue, he said:

> "It is precisely on the basis of this principle of repatriation of all prisoners of war that our side firmly maintain that the detaining side should ensure that no coercive means whatsoever be employed against all the prisoners of war in its custody to obstruct their returning home. . . . The Korean and Chinese side does not acknowledge that there are

. . . **March 30, 1953.** Chinese Communist Premier Chou En-Lai announces Communist side will agree to exchange all prisoners on voluntary repatriation basis. . . . .

prisoners of war who are allegedly unwilling to be repatriated. Therefore the question of the so-called 'forced repatriation' or 'repatriation by force' does not exist at all, and we have always opposed this assertion. . . ."

In short, war as usual. The meaning of this statement was that to settle the war, the U.N. must return all Communist prisoners, no matter what their desires, to Communist control. At this point, in early April, there had been more U.N. casualties since the repatriation impasse had begun in mid-1951 than there were U.N. prisoners in Communist control. The U.N. negotiation position was therefore becoming more costly with each passing day. The U.N. insisted on the right to choose because there was good reason to believe tens of thousands of the 100,000 or so Communist prisoners it held would refuse to go back to Communist control. The American negotiators insisted that there would be no forced repatriation and this was unacceptable to the Communists. The North Korean general's stalemate meant that the mainly Americans, British, and South Korean prisoners, now thought to number about 13,000, would have to remain in Communist prison camps until a resolution of the issue was reached. Unfortunately, some of the American prisoners, such as a U.S. Marine Corps pilot shot down over North Korea and later interviewed by Major James Angus MacDonald, Jr., were in desperate need of care:

"Captain Gerald Fink was flying an F4U Corsair on an interdiction mission on August, 1951. He was attacking vehicles on a main supply route near Sagaru-ri located southwest of Wonsan [eastern North Korea] and about eighteen miles from the east coast. Captain Fink came in low, intent on his target and unmindful of the hail of small-arms fire that rose to meet him. The throttle controls were hit and so severely damaged that the throttle quadrant came off in his hands, and he lost control of his engine.

One of the pilots heard someone say, 'I'm hit, I'm on fire.' It was 10:58 A.M.

"When Captain Fink attempted to bail out, the canopy jammed crookedly on its tracks making it impossible for him to get free from the stricken aircraft. Fink punched the canopy with his fist causing it to blow off and at the same time inflicting several cuts to his hands. He finally bailed out at a low altitude and after three swings in his parachute, he hit the ground.

"North Koreans manning nearby positions opened fire and he was struck in the left knee by a bullet from a submachine gun. The Koreans left their position to rush the Marine, and when he reached for his revolver, one soldier stuck him in the mouth with the butt of his rifle and knocked out two upper front teeth. . . . The soldiers also deliberately broke his arm with a butt stroke. . . .

"The enemy took Captain Fink to a hole in the side of a hill where he was kept for about three days. During that time he was given no food, water or medical attention. . . .

"After removal from the hole, Captain Fink was bound with his elbows crooked over a tree branch across his back and his hands tied tightly in front of him. His three North Korean guards dragged him along through several small villages en route to Wonsan. He was unshaven, unwashed, befouled and ill-smelling. The final humiliation occurred during the day and a half in which he lay outside a shattered building on a street in Wonsan. A virtual procession of Korean women spat on him and then squatted and urinated on him as he lay helpless. His flight suit rapidly took on the aspects of a Korean latrine. . . .

"After the ordeal at Wonsan, the Marine was taken on an overland trek towards Pyongyang. En route, he was temporarily held at a place called 'Wu's' near Yangdok. Captain Wu, who had lost his testicles to an unfriendly bullet, bore little affection for United Nations pilots. The

Communist demonstrated his attitude during the ten days of Captain Fink's stay by administering repeated beatings with a .45 caliber automatic as he tried to pry information concerning naval organization from his captive. . . ."

Several days later, Fink joined a group of British Commandos that had been captured. All were herded to the North Korean capital for more interrogations at a place that became known to the British and American prisoners as Pak's:

"At Pak's, the enemy singled out the Marine to be interrogated first while the Commandos looked on. His interrogator was a mountainous Russian woman so large across her posterior that she required the seating space of two chairs. She wore a filmy blue dress and cheap beads and earrings. To make matters more ludicrous, she wore Korean shoes which Fink later described as Korean 'boondockers,' a Marine term for field shoes.

"When the Russian behemoth asked through her interpreter why he had come to Korea, Fink replied, 'To kill Communists.' He was promptly kicked and beaten with sticks expertly wielded by the North Korean guards. After several minutes of beating, Fink was again interrogated, although as much time was devoted to lecturing him on his inhumanity as was devoted to questioning him about military matters.

"The Russian inquisitor accused all Americans of bestiality and of murdering women and children. Fink noticed three blond hairs that were growing from the tip of her bulbous nose. As the interrogation continued, he became fascinated by the hairs. The fascination grew into an obsession, until, unable to restrain himself, he leaned forward and neatly plucked one of the hairs off her nose. The North Korean guards immediately set upon him with punches, kicks, and severe blows with their clubs. The

[British] commandos, who were looking on, thought the incident amusing, but they were concerned over possible repercussions. Fink spent the next three days in a vermin infested hole in solitary confinement.

"It was at Pak's that Captain Fink first saw a man die from dysentery. One of the Royal Marines with Quartermaster Sergeant Day's party was unable to withstand the combination of starvation and dysentery. Fink helped Day bury the corpse, and the latter described the act as, 'Again, ordinary you may say, but you see, most of the POW's at Pak's were in such a weak condition it was an effort to do anything.'

"The weakened condition of the prisoners was the result of brutal treatment, bare subsistence, sickness, lack of medicine and medical care, hard labor, and the constant threats, beatings and interrogations. In addition to the Royal Marine who died, an Air Force lieutenant colonel, an Army major and two Army captains died of malnutrition, dysentery and, in at least one case, severe beatings by the enemy.

"Daily routine at Pak's consisted of digging bomb shelters, carrying water for the Koreans, chopping wood and carrying it into camp and carrying supplies and rice from Pak's Place into the local town of Yong Song, digging trenches, and building mud shacks for the Koreans. The work was accomplished despite the poor condition of prisoners, and the Koreans threatened and beat the POW's with little or no provocation."

Major MacDonald also interviewed a number of Americans who were held in Chinese-run camps. He concluded:

"The North Koreans treated their prisoners cruelly, but their brutality was physical. The Chinese introduced a more insidious form of cruelty. With them, physical violence was less general but more purposeful and it was liberally spiced with mental pressure. The North Koreans made token efforts to extract military information from their prisoners taking more pleasure in maltreating than in exploiting them. The Chinese Communists were more effective in their intelligence activities. In addition, they made an intensive effort to indoctrinate their prisoners of war or to gain a propaganda advantage. . . ."

MacDonald then contrasted the harsh conditions at Pak's Place, a North Korean facility, with the more relaxed routine at a Chinese camp, Kanggye:

"The daily routine was boring though not particularly arduous. Prisoners arose at 7 A.M. and either took a short walk or performed light calisthenics. They washed their faces and hands, and at 8 A.M., representatives from each squad drew the appropriate number of rations from the kitchen. Food was cooked by the Chinese and the diet was essentially the same as that provided the Communist soldiers consisting of singular items such as sorghum seed, bean curd, soya bean flour, or cracked corn and on certain special occasions such as Christmas or Lunar New Year, the prisoners received small portions of rice, boiled fatty pork, candy and peanuts. The prisoners were told that they were being fed because the Chinese were good; no reference was made to international agreements or the responsibilities of captors for their captives; they were fed simply because the Chinese were good.

"After breakfast the prisoners were either marched to the barn which served as a communal lecture hall, or they were required to conduct informal political discussions within their own huts. Squad leaders were held responsible for proper discussions by their squads of assigned topics in Marxian dialectical materialism. There seems to have been little or no direct organized opposition to the indoctrination; indeed there seems to have been little opportunity for it since study periods were mandatory; the POW's did not have the option of refusing to attend or to participate in lectures and discussions.

"On rare days a noon meal was served, although frequently only two meals were prepared and the noon meal was omitted. After an hour set aside for resting, the afternoon lecture or discussion began and lasted for two hours. The supper meal was generally served at 5 P.M. when camp housekeeping details were completed. The prisoners retired at about 7 P.M. Holiday routine prevailed only on Christmas and New Year's, so that Saturdays and Sundays passed like any other day. It is evident from the carefully established routine that the Chinese wanted the POW's to concentrate on their enforced studies. The curriculum was more intensive than most college courses. From the reports of other camps, the treatment of most POW's at Kanggye was less brutal than that accorded any group of prisoners during this period. Yet this leniency was coldly calculated to neutralize possible resisters and to convert those who could be bent to the Communists' will. At the same time, when viewed objectively, many of United Nations personnel at Kanggye were comparatively well treated and were fed as well as their captors although all of the prisoners were suffering varying degrees of malnutrition from lack of a properly balanced diet.

"Chinese doctors provided medications of a far lower standard than would be found in a normal field first aid station. Aspirin pills were a common remedy; the next most common service seems to have been removing black, frozen toes without sedation. Some of the sickest personnel disappeared from camp; those who remained were told the others were en route to a hospital.

"Meanwhile, those who remained at Kanggye were

exposed to the continuing indoctrination program of the Chinese. At the very outset the POW's were informed that the most progressive among them would be taken south to the front lines and released. This announcement was undoubtedly made to foster cooperation, and it succeeded, at least to the extent that many prisoners vied with each other to make speeches and to produce articles suitable for the camp newspaper. Successful authors received cigarettes as a reward for their literary efforts, courtesy of the Chinese People's Volunteers. The paper, 'New Life,' consisted generally of one or two pages which reproduced the hand-printed articles written by the prisoners. Six issues were produced during January 1951. . . . By their own admission the Chinese were able to secure contributions of articles from only a small percentage of the prisoners, though any contributions represented a victory for the Communists.

"The following article is illustrative of the type which was suitable to the Communists and was published in the camp newspaper. Entitled 'We Were Paid Killers,' this article, written by a U.S. Marine private . . . appeared in the fifth edition of 'New Life' published on January 22, 1951, at Kanggye. The text read as follows:

" 'Since I was liberated, I've been given time to just think and analyze this Korean problem. Often I've asked myself "Were we paid killers?" "Are these Korean people really our enemy?" "Why am I here?" These questions have brought me to the conclusion that the American capitalists have made us nothing short of paid killers. But we were ignorant of the fact and we followed the capitalists without asking ourselves "Why?" I am sure none of us would kill a fellow American in cold blood. But we have killed these innocent people just because MacArthur and Truman said, "they are our enemy." In reality they are a peace loving people and it is only the capitalists' lust for more power and money that had caused bloodshed. And we were the cannon fodder for their willful desires. But now we are enlightened to these facts. I believe none of us will be fooled again.'

"The young author of 'We Were Paid Killers' did not serve the Communists' purpose for long. He became an aggressive 'reactionary' and on several occasions was put in solitary confinement in rat-infested holes. He never did fully regain the trust of his fellow captives, however, even though he had become a 'red hot reactionary.' "

Some stories about Americans held captive in North Korea made their way to the United States. Indications about collaboration with the Communists were circulated by media sources with a leftist orientation and were generally disbelieved, most likely because there were other stories, complete with photographic proof, concerning Communist mistreatment of Americans in their care. As the Americans advanced up the Peninsula in the fall of 1950, they discovered undeniable evidence of atrocities. The bodies of a number of U.S. troops taken by the North Koreans were found in shallow graves, their hands bound behind their backs, and bullet holes in the backs of their heads. Thus, the common idea about alleged collaboration was that severe coercion, maybe torture, was being used and therefore any statements made by Americans in Communist hands could be dismissed. This was reinforced by a continuing series of stories detailing some shocking events. These were the product of a U.N. war crimes investigation. One of the investigations dealt with the grisly fate of a squad of marines in 1951:

"Korean War Crime #185, Marine Patrol. Ten marines from the 1st Marine Division went on a reconnaissance patrol near Nakchon Dong on 29 January 1951. They never returned from this mission. In March 1951, checking on a

National Police report, a patrol from the 2nd ROK Division found their bodies, together with those of ten Republic of Korea Army soldiers, four National Police, and one Korean civilian. These corpses were stripped naked with the hands bound behind them, and the physical appearance of the remains revealed that the decedents had either been bayonetted in the back and chest or had their skulls crushed with clubs.

"Interrogation of native villagers indicated that these Americans were captured about 30 January and held prisoners until their murder on 5 February 1951.

"Two North Korean lieutenants, discovered among captured Communist prisoners, have confessed to participation in this crime. Although their statements were recorded at different times and places, the factual data is the same. They relate that their commanding officer told them to prepare to execute the prisoners secretly. For this purpose, they decided to use bayonets. Accordingly, the graves were dug in advance, then the victims were led forth individually, stripped, bound and ordered to sit on the ground. In this position, each man was used for bayonet practice, and if death came too slowly or resistance was offered, his head was smashed with a rifle butt. Blood stains were swept from the ground and the bodies buried."

Attracting less attention in the U.S. were the more numerous stories of South Koreans who had suffered under North Korean control. Atrocities against the southerners were beyond doubt the largest single category of war crimes. Additionally, South Koreans constituted the largest number of U.N. prisoners under North Korean control. And they made up another group that was highly significant to the stalled negotiations. Many of the Korean prisoners in U.N. hands were southerners who had been forced into the North Korean Army and were now refusing repatriation to Communist control. In the spring of 1953 U.N.

leaders who read the war crimes investigations knew how and under what conditions some of these southerners joined the Communists:

"Korean War Crime #56. Forcible Conscription at Tong Tang-ni. Many of our enemy prisoners of war are discovered to be South Koreans who were conscripted into the communist armies against their wishes. The procedure followed at Tong Tang-ni demonstrates one manner in which this was accomplished. On 2 October 1950, all the young men of the village were assembled by the North Korean Security Police and given the choice of entering the North Korean army or being imprisoned. Approximately forty men refused to volunteer and were jailed. Soon thereafter, the prisoners' hands were tied behind their backs and they were divided into two groups. One group was taken to the river bank and shot to death by their five guards. The other suffered a like fate after being lined up on the edge of a large pit."

Although the war during the spring of 1953 largely resembled more of the same, there were some subtle differences that were noted by U.S. leaders. On the ground, the Chinese began a number of offensives designed to gain a piece of choice territory, usually one with a militarily significant vantage point. These efforts, beginning in May, were much like those of 1952, mostly aimed at the South Koreans and all of a limited objective nature. As a matter of concern to the Americans, the Communists were now using more artillery support. In April the Communists had fired 51,690 artillery rounds, a figure that almost doubled to 99,340 rounds in May. The shock was that this number, in turn, skyrocketed in June, achieving a threefold

Butcher's aftermath. *Civilian victims of a North Korean Army atrocity, Chonju, South Korea.*

increase: some 329,130 rounds fired at the Allies. Together with the fact that Communist prisoners were being captured in an increasingly well fed condition, this rise in Communist firepower gave the U.N. field commanders the sobering indication of just how ineffective the American air interdiction campaign was. The Communists were clearly able to bring more and more supplies to the front.

On the other hand, the U.N. airmen were doing much better in air-to-air combat, although the reason for the change was a bit murky. There had been a widely advertised American campaign offering monetary rewards for the Communist pilots who would bring their MiGs to a U.N. airfield, land them safely, and surrender. Shortly after this broadcast, the North Korean leader, Kim Il Sung, took to the airwaves with his own message. The U.S. Air Force historian, Lieutenant Colonel Robert Futrell, recounts:

"In an unusual message to North Korea's 'air heroes,' Kim Il Sung promised that the North Korean Air Force would have a greater responsibility for air defense and exhorted Korean airmen to strengthen their military discipline and protect their equipment. During the early months of 1953 most MiG's engaged by Sabres had borne the plain red stars of Soviet Russia, but after May 8 most MiG's sighted bore Chinese Communist and North Korean insignia. The pilots who now flew the MiG's . . . were willing to engage in combat, but they had far more enthusiasm than ability. General [Mark] Clark thought it significant that 'the Communist MiG pilots who were permitted to fly after the (reward) offer was made were the worst of the whole Korean war.'

"For the Sabre pilots the months of May and June 1953 were reminiscent of the famed 'Marianas Turkey Shoot' of World War II, when Japan's naval airmen had been blasted from the skies in phenomenal numbers. At the same time in which the MiG airmen were eager but unskilled, the Sabre pilots were always 'tigers' and were displaying superior tactical and gunnery skills. Ever since the early days of combat the Sabres had emphasized high-speed cruising in the target area, but now they began to employ up to 98 percent of their power while awaiting

. . . **June 6, 1953.** South Korean President Syngman Rhee says his government would not approve of an "unacceptable" truce . . . **June 14, 1953.** Communists launch biggest offensive in more than two years pushing South Korean troops back as much as eight miles on east central front . . . .

combat. The higher speeds reduced the time the Sabres could stay on patrols, but they had important offensive and defensive benefits. If a MiG were sighted, the Sabre's rate of closure was higher, and if a MiG attacked, the MiG's rate of closure was slower. In combat between 8 and 31 May the Sabres sighted 1,507 MiG's, engaged 537 of them, and destroyed 56 at a combat loss of only one Sabre."

Some put the increased American effectiveness down to the reward, others believed it was a matter of international dynamics, and a third group concluded that revised U.S. tactics accounted for the lopsided encounters. Those who cited the monetary rationale assumed that only politically reliable Communist pilots had been sent aloft, producing a large proportion of less capable airmen for the Americans to deal with. Another interpretation put forth the idea that Moscow's hopeful comments of March were genuine and the Soviets were putting pressure on the Chinese and North Koreans by withdrawing their own and Polish pilots from air combat, forcing the Asian partners to come to terms at the truce talks. Possibly, the clear-cut U.S. air superiority was the result of a combination of factors—it has never been completely explained, and neither has what happened next.

On May 22, 1953, the United States transmitted a serious threat to China. President Eisenhower authorized his Secretary of State, John Foster Dulles, to relay a message to the Chinese and Russians through the government of India. The American President warned that if the stalemate continued, the U.S. was willing to attack the previously untouched Communist sanctuary bases in Manchuria. Three days later, there was a change in the character of the truce talks. The Communist negotiator

... **June 20, 1953.** Communist high command demands assurance South Korea will abide by truce; armistice negotiations recessed "indefinitely." . . . .

became forthcoming, indicating he was authorized to make a deal. By May 27, although a number of details were still to be worked out, rapid progress was evident. By June 8 there was a fundamentally agreeable document that only missed some details prior to its approval by both sides. The Communists, winning the right to conduct a longer persuasion period in front of those prisoners in U.N. hands who refused repatriation, would abide by U.N. conditions: no forced repatriation and Communist "explainers" had to conduct pleas to their former soldiers on neutral ground and under the control of neutral observers. It was an unambiguous American negotiation victory. For fifteen months, Washington and the U.S. military negotiators had not budged. America had proven more patient, more enduring, and more willing to sacrifice for its principles than had the Communists.

Ten days later, an anticlimactic event threatened prospects for the cease-fire, but President Eisenhower's decisive intervention recouped the chance for an end to the fighting. Fearing the U.S. would abandon it after a cease-fire, the South Korean government had pressed American authorities for increased economic and military aid and had indicated a growing distaste for the deal being negotiated with the Communists. The southerners continually reminded U.S. officials that the original American objective had been a free, independent, and unified Korea. On June 18 a disruptive deed replaced these comments and requests. ROK guards encouraged the escape of 25,000 Communist prisoners who had indicated a preference for the U.N. side, Koreans who would likely reject repatriation. Predictably, two days later, the Communist negotiators walked out of the talks. They had been

. . . **June 28, 1953.** General Clark proposes resumption of truce negotiations promising all in his power to ensure South Korea's Army will observe armistice . . . **July 8, 1953.** Communists agree to proceed with truce talks on basis of General Clark's assurances . . . .

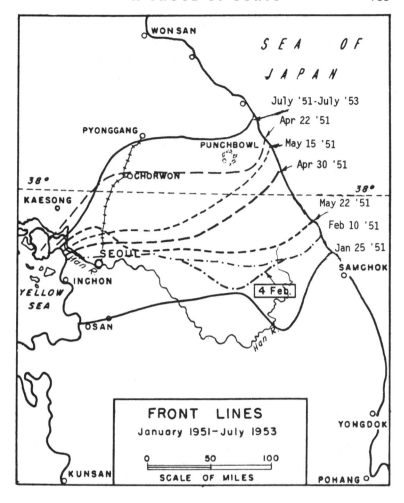

WON SAN

SEA OF

JAPAN

July '51-July '53

Apr 22 '51

PYONGGANG

PUNCHBOWL

May 15 '51

CHORWON

Apr 30 '51

38°   38°

KAESONG

May 22 '51

Feb 10 '51

SEOUL

Jan 25 '51

Han R.

SAMCHOK

INCHON

4 Feb.

YELLOW

SEA

OSAN

Han R.

FRONT LINES

January 1951 – July 1953

YONGDOK

0   50   100

KUNSAN   SCALE OF MILES   POHANG

robbed of the chance to persuade this group of their former soldiers to return to the fold and understandably assumed the Americans could not guarantee the behavior of the government of South Korea.

Eisenhower moved swiftly. Writing a searing message to the South Korean President, Syngman Rhee, a damning recital of all the past agreements and promises the ROK government had broken with its reckless action, Eisenhower made it unmistakably clear that South Korea would be indeed abandoned if its government persisted in undercutting American policies. Additionally, he sent his personal representative to Seoul to ensure President Rhee got the full message. Just as the Communists had caved in to a firmly held U.S. position, so too did the President of the Republic of Korea. On July 10 talks with the Communists were resumed. On July 27 the truce agreement, a pledge by both sides to stop firing, was signed.

That day, on the front lines, the waiting for war's end began. First Lieutenant Robert J. Gerard recalls:

"July 27, 1953, started out as a rather quiet day on line with the 3rd Battalion, 224th Infantry Regiment, 40th Division. We were located on the west edge of the Punchbowl, near a place we called 'Luke's Castle,' a nasty little piece of ground which had changed hands a number of times as a result of probes and combat raids. Assaults on the 'Castle' were designed to punish the enemy, but not to seize and hold ground forward of our established positions. It was perhaps the only point along the miles of battle positions that brought the American and North Korean forces within one or two hundred yards of each other.

"July 27 was an important day because the official cease fire was to take place at 10 P.M. that night. No contacts with the enemy were reported during the day. Daylight patrols were limited to setting up ambush positions just a short distance in front of the main line of resistance (MLR). The generally quiet day was punctuated from time to time by a burst of small arms fire or the scheduled program of Harassing and Interdiction fires

. . . **July 11, 1953.** Syngman Rhee promises to collaborate in armistice . . . .

planned for the Division artillery and the mortars. In exchange, we received our own share of sporadic incoming rounds and some occasional small arms fire.

"As twilight approached, there was a sense of excitement in the air. We had received strict instructions that all weapons firing was to cease promptly by 10 P.M. At about 8 P.M., as it grew dark, the occasional exchange of fire picked up in tempo. Rifle fire was reinforced with the chattering of automatic weapons. The mortars were reinforced with artillery which swooshed overhead on its way to some unseen enemy. Recoilless rifles positioned along the line added their ear-piercing blasts to the crescendo. The Quad 50s [four .50-caliber machine guns mounted on a half-track vehicle] assigned to support us laced the North Korean positions with a stream of fire. Both sides had picked up the pace and by 9:30 P.M., the exchange was at a peak. It was as if both sides were under heavy attack and were shooting desperately to keep from being overrun. The air was thick with the acrid smell of gunpowder mixed with clouds of dirt and dust. The sky was illuminated with one flare after another.

"At about 9:45 P.M., the firing began to fall off in reverse sequence. First, the artillery slowed; then the mortars, then the small arms. At 9:55 P.M., firing was limited to an occasional short burst from an automatic weapon. After a few more single rifle shots, it became deadly quiet. The only remaining noise was the whispering sound of a final parachute flare, casting an eerie glow over our positions and whispering, almost mournfully, as it clung to its fading light.

"At first, no one spoke. Then voices could be heard up and down the line. Nervous laughter. Someone lit a ciga-

---

. . . **July 27, 1953.** Truce signed. Cease-fire begins. Korean War ends.

rette. More talk. More laughter. The flash of a Zippo lighter. There was a sense of calm; a sense of relief. In the dark, you couldn't see it, but you could feel it. I looked up at the sky. The stars were crystal clear, sparkling against a deep blue background. I thought, 'It's good to be alive. No one should die on a night like this.' "

The Korean War was over.

THE MEANING OF
IT ALL

FROM AN IMMEDIATE postwar wave of heated controversy in
the United States, the Korean War, despite its importance,
dropped from public view within only three years. It was almost as if the episode was some embarrassing and dark family
story, better ignored than discussed. By 1956 it was already a
seldom recounted and rarely analyzed conflict and it has remained that way ever since. Yet few American wars have so
heavily influenced subsequent events or so shaped American
behavior. The war catapulted a Third World state into a role of
great international import, ensured the industrialized West
would confront the Communist East with an enormous peacetime military establishment, and provoked the United States
into abandoning a century-and-a-half peacetime tradition of
avoiding "entangling alliances." For Koreans, the promise of
unification was not just briefly postponed, it has become in-

creasingly remote even after the Cold War ended. Last and certainly not least, this ill-remembered conflict is proving to be one of America's most unselfish and unambiguously principled armed conflicts.

In the United States the aftermath of the conflict brought a profound sense of waste and frustration for about two years. The east-west cease-fire line, called the Demilitarized Zone, straddled the 38th parallel. The U.N. had given up some terrain south of the prewar line of demarcation in the western part of the Peninsula. But, to the east, it had gained ground. There, the line of opposing trenches was well north of the parallel, yielding a net wartime territorial gain for the Republic of Korea. To most Americans, the added real estate was clearly not worth the cost. They quickly became accustomed to hearing this expensive conflict described as "the only war the U.S. lost." Indeed, the war was costly. The U.N. suffered over 500,000 casualties, including 94,000 dead, 33,629 of whom were Americans. The U.S. also suffered 103,284 wounded and 5,178 missing or captured. The Communists were believed to have sustained three times the losses, an estimated 1.5 million casualties.

The sticking point of the truce talks, the matter of repatriation, continued to plague both sides well after the guns fell silent. The physical transfer was unremarkable, managed largely according to what had been agreed. The opportunities to voluntarily return to one's country or to refuse repatriation, and the chance to reconsider the choice, were conducted under the watchful eyes of neutral authorities. In all, the Communists turned over 13,444 U.N. prisoners, including 8,321 South Koreans and 3,746 Americans. However, only 6,670 of the Chinese prisoners in U.N. hands were handed over; 14,247 refused repatriation, most choosing to live in Taiwan under the Nationalist Chinese government. A higher percentage of North Koreans opted to return home, 75,823 of the 83,501. However, to the 12,000 or so remaining in the South, one might add the

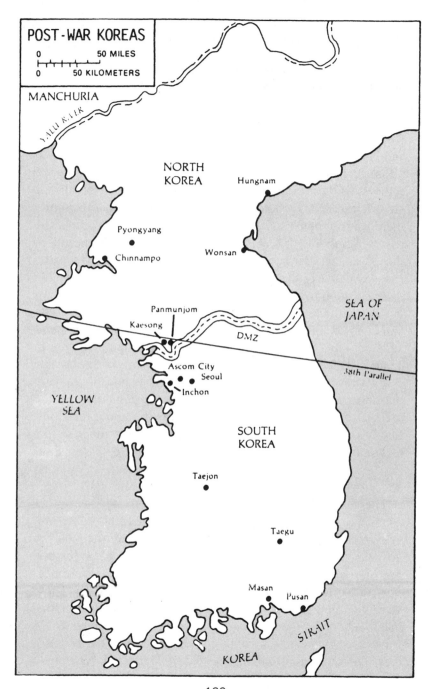

POST-WAR KOREAS

0 — 50 MILES
0 — 50 KILOMETERS

MANCHURIA

YALU RIVER

NORTH
KOREA

Hungnam

Pyongyang

Chinnampo

Wonsan

SEA OF
JAPAN

Panmunjom

Kaesong

DMZ

38th Parallel

Ascom City

Seoul

Inchon

YELLOW
SEA

SOUTH
KOREA

Taejon

Taegu

Masan

Pusan

STRAIT

KOREA

189

estimated 25,000 released by the South Korean government prior to the truce agreement.

The most unpleasant and sensational postwar story in America centered on the conduct and choices of a distinct handful of Americans who were among the U.N. prisoners in Communist hands. In all, there were 347 of the almost 13,800 total who refused repatriation, deciding to remain with their Communist captors. Of these "nonrepatriates," there were 325 Koreans, 21 Americans, and one soldier from the United Kingdom. While there was not much speculation in the Western press about the reason thousands of Communist soldiers refused repatriation, there was massive public concern about the U.N. nonrepatriates, particularly the Americans. Mostly, the behavior of the 347 was put down to their fear of retaliation over their collaboration with Communist officials. Interrogation of those who chose to be exchanged clearly indicated some reprehensible actions of betrayal on the part of the nonrepatriates. In some instances, these cowardly acts cost some of their brave countrymen their lives, and the betrayers would have every reason to expect vengeance should they return home. But the press also exhibited great zeal in speculating about the Communists' prisoner indoctrination and behavior modification techniques, a phenomenon dubbed by reporters as "brainwashing." Treason, betrayal, and a new and sinister art of mind control—all became fodder for lurid journalism.

The general sense of defeat, futility, and waste was further advanced by diplomatic events shortly after the cease-fire. While the armistice and prisoner exchange were the result of difficult negotiations by the military authorities of both sides, the subsequent and promised political negotiations were conducted by the war's participants at the ministerial level. These were held in Geneva, Switzerland in April 1954. Nations that had fought under the U.N. banner proposed an all-Korea, U.N.-supervised free election leading to unification of the two Koreas. The Communists flatly rejected this proposal, refusing to acknowledge the concept of proportional representation. To them, the two-thirds of all Koreans living in the South, under the government of the Republic of Korea, should have no more influence than the one-third living under Communist control. Additionally, they would not accept the U.N. as an impartial body. After less than two months of unseemly bickering, the deadlocked diplomats gave up and went home.

Demagogic politicians stoked the fires of America's frustration with the war. These worthies sought notoriety by raising dark thoughts of subversion and conspiracy in high places to explain the war's unsatisfactory results. In many instances, these public figures pointed an accusing finger at the nation's Department of Defense. Thirty-five years after the guns fell silent, one of that department's historians explained some of the reasons for the immediate postwar dissatisfaction and characterized the political outcome:

"The Korean War was not a test of U.S. capability on the scale of World War II; the partial mobilization required little more than a quarter of the military manpower raised in 1940–45 and a much smaller industrial mobilization. But the unity of purpose and effort that had marked the earlier war was conspicuously absent in 1950–53. Because it was a 'police action,' an undeclared war in a faraway and relatively unknown country, because its limited objectives did not include surrender by the North Koreans and later the Chinese, because it incurred disproportionately heavy casualties, and because it dragged on without prospect of either victory or termination, the war could not begin to command the unity of national purpose and whole-hearted public support that World War II had evoked.

"Already overburdened by the demands of fighting a war abroad and having to cope with a host of other exigent problems, the secretaries of defense soon found themselves caught up in some of the most bitter and divisive domestic political battles of 20th century U.S. history. The vitriolic, venomous fulminations of such ultrapartisans as Republican Senators [Joseph R.] McCarthy, [William E.] Jenner, and [Kenneth S.] Wherry far exceeded the bounds of legitimate criticism. Their arraignment of the Defense Department included its military as well as civilian leadership and extended eventually even to allegations of conspiracy and internal subversion. The conduct of the war, its problematical outcome and the heavy toll of American lives afforded other opposition elements opportunities to make political capital out of issues on which the administration was vulnerable. The firing of General MacArthur excited a storm of protest in which the secretary of defense and the department came under intense attack. . . ."

While the Department of Defense was the object of much of this venom, the State Department and the United Nations absorbed a considerable share as well. Most of the sparks were launched during purposely sensationalized hearings on Capitol Hill, forums where politicians could ask disgruntled military leaders questions that were sure to draw exaggerated attention and subsequent recriminations. About one year after the cease-fire, in August 1954, a Senate subcommittee questioned General Mark Clark:

SENATOR PATRICK A. MCCARRAN: Was it your judgement or is it your judgement now that, had we crossed the Yalu River at the time the Chinese came across, that might have triggered a third world war?

CLARK: . . . I do not think it would have started World War III, nor do I think, when I was in command and had I bombed the [Manchurian] bases, which I would like to have done, and the airfields from which the enemy derived his source of power, that would have dragged us into World War III. I do not think you can drag the Soviets into a world war except at a time and place of their own choosing. They have been doing too well in the "Cold War."

Before this same subcommittee, Clark, Van Fleet, and General George E. Stratemeyer, MacArthur's senior Air Force officer, railed against President Truman's limited war policies. Some thought restrictions on bombing Manchuria were responsible for the U.N. inability to bring the war to a victorious conclusion. Others cited the prohibition on the use of Chinese Nationalist troops as being a contributing factor to a no-win war:

CLARK: Once our leaders, our authorized leaders, the President and Congress, decide that fight we must, in my opinion we should fight without any holds barred whatsoever. We should fight to win, and we should not go in for a limited war where we put our limited manpower against the unlimited hordes of Communist manpower which they are willing to expend lavishly, and do. They have no value for human life or respect for it at all. If fight we must, let's go in there and shoot the works for victory with everything at our disposal.

VAN FLEET: I never understood why we did not use Chiang Kai-shek's divisions. Looking on it today, it was a terrible mistake, because it would have given them wonderful training, a battle test, to develop Chiang's army and to know which of his generals are good in combat and what the Nationalist troops can really do. Even today we do not know that answer.

STRATEMEYER: It [the restriction against bombing Manchurian targets] is contrary to everything that every military commander that I have been associated with or from all of our history—he has never been in a position where he could not win the war he started to win. This is not American. That is not American. . . .

During this same series of hearings, some military witnesses were maneuvered into suggesting the Truman administration had missed great opportunities in failing to decisively defeat Communism. In a play on the 1951 "wrong time, wrong place, wrong war" statement by the chairman of the Joint Chiefs of Staff, General of the Army Omar N. Bradley, several officers, known critics of Truman's policies, were asked a leading question. Neither the officers nor their inquisitors bothered to explain the original nature of the chairman's statement. Bradley had been referring to General MacArthur's proposal to expand the war geographically and employ weapons of mass destruction after China had entered the conflict. And these critics perhaps did not know that Bradley had been alone among the country's senior officers in objecting to the exclusion of Korea from a list of strategic lands prior to the war. Given the context of the questions posed in 1954, General Bradley would have undoubtedly agreed with the response given by Truman's military detractors:

SENATOR TERRY M. CARPENTER: Was Korea the wrong war in the wrong place and at the wrong time?

VAN FLEET: Well, certainly not. I have often made a statement that it was the right war at the right place and the right time against the right enemy and with the right allies, thinking of the Koreans as very worthy friends. . . .

CARPENTER: Was Korea the wrong war in the wrong place and at the wrong time?

ADMIRAL C. TURNER JOY: Quite the contrary. It was a war of deep significance in a battle area which held many advantages for the United Nations forces. Furthermore, it was very timely from the standpoint of resisting Communist aggression. With the excellent bases in Japan, with the capabilities of flying carrier based planes over the entire peninsula, and with a coast line that lent itself admirably to bombardment missions in support of the Army, the Navy could not have fought in a more favorable distant area from the United States.

As the Truman administration's war policies were being challenged, members of the new Republican administration were claiming credit for ending the conflict Americans had found so agonizingly distasteful. Eisenhower's Secretary of State, John Foster Dulles, was unequivocal in his belief that the President's May 22, 1953, threat delivered to the Chinese and Russians ended the war. In January 1954 the Secretary offered this explanation of why the Communists ended their resistance to the military truce and agreed to the cease-fire:

"... the aggressor, already thrown back to and behind his place of beginning, was faced with the possibility that the fighting might, to his own great peril, soon spread beyond the limits and methods he had selected."

A part of this threat, the idea of extending the boundaries of the war, was repeated immediately after the cease-fire agreement in the form of a possible U.N. contingency should hostilities be resumed. It is significant that Secretary Dulles spoke of geographic extension and new "methods," the latter being an unmistakable code word for the likely use of nuclear weapons. America's allies clearly agreed with the notion of geographic expansion, but would not assent to the employment of mass-destruction weapons. A week after the signing, the participating members of the U.N.'s effort in Korea issued a warning to the Communist side. It was contained in a single paragraph of the U.N. Command's report to the Security Council:

"We declare again our faith in the principles and purposes of the United Nations, our consciousness of the continuing responsibilities in Korea, and our determination in good faith to seek a settlement of the Korean problem. We affirm, in the interests of world peace, that if there is a renewal of the armed attack, challenging again the principles of the United Nations, we should again be united and prompt to resist. The consequences of such a breach of the armistice would be so grave that, in all probability, it would not be possible to confine hostilities within the frontiers of Korea."

For many Americans, this unpalatable war demanded assurances that future conflicts would not be conducted with the same methods President Truman had chosen. They believed there must be no more fighting at the time, at the place, and with the means the Communists preferred. The unsophisticated nature of the Korean War, the dependence on infantry rifles, grenades, and even bayonets, put the U.S. at a disadvantage, unable to use its great technological superiority. In some quarters, particularly among the Republican officials now occupying positions of power in Washington, there was determination to pursue wholly new military policies. Air Force General William W. Momyer described the resulting policy dispute that erupted not long after the shooting had stopped in Korea:

"After the agony and expense of Korea, an understandably popular position was that we would never fight, nor should we prepare to fight, another war like Korea. Adding to the popularity of this position was the fact that it could be used to justify a reduction in defense force expenditures. If a limited war should break out, proponents said, nuclear weapons could end it quickly. The way to prevent such wars would be to maintain military and political pressure against potential instigators. If the outside support for a limited conflict were neutralized, the conflict itself would soon die for lack of weapons and other resources. Most airmen consented to the idea that nuclear weapons should be the basis of our defense strategies. But the Army and Navy maintained that limited conflict was most likely and that limited wars would, at least initially, be fought with conventional weapons."

This argument effectively overshadowed and then replaced the controversy about the conduct of the Korean War itself, and by 1956 disputes were centered on future policies. There were at least two reasons for this phenomenon. First, there were virtually no defenders of Truman's military policies—no one to claim there had been any sort of American or U.N. victory in Korea. Second, there was an unstated but near-universal agreement not to speak about the Korean War, because it was increasingly viewed as an aberration, an atypical event that would never be repeated. There was a widely held understanding that a new approach had to be taken in international security affairs. Arguments revolved around which new methods would be more likely to succeed. Policies that came to be identified with the U.S. Air Force and the Republican party came to be known as "massive retaliation." The Army and Navy, often with support from some members of the Democratic party, favored less deterministic policies. Their ideas evolved into a policy called "flexible response." This was a concept fostered by the last wartime Eighth Army commander, General Maxwell Taylor, and later published in his 1959 book, *The Uncertain Trumpet*. Flexible response featured the possible use of nuclear weapons, but mainly advocated new-style American ground and air forces, agile legions of great tactical and strategic mobility possessing awesome firepower. This idea was based on the belief that the Communists would have to be contested in limited, "brushfire" wars in the Third World, because the policy of massive retaliation provided no answer to the gradual absorption of the developing nations into the Soviet orbit. Flexible response was eagerly adopted by an aspiring Senator, John F. Kennedy of Massachusetts.

While Americans might fume with one another over coming

defense policies, they were largely in agreement about a dramatic change in the global balance of power. A new major power had been born in the early 1950s. China, the chaotic, hunger-plagued, and backward country that drew little more than pity in the first half of the twentieth century, had now earned respect—even fear. In 1950 the Chinese Red Army had advanced beyond the nation's borders and had literally thrown the armed forces of the United States out of North Korea. With unlimited manpower and a growing industrial base, Communist China added a new dimension and source of apparent strength to the Marxist cause.

The war not only created an ominous new major actor on the world scene, it fostered two dramatic breaks with long-established American traditions. For more than a century and a half, the United States had energetically dismantled its armed forces immediately after they had been employed. But, long after the firing had died in Korea, America steadfastly maintained a powerful army, navy, and air force. For the first time in its history, the United States was armed to the teeth in peacetime. And, in another precedent-breaking reversal, the United States enthusiastically sponsored a globe-girding mutual defense network. Ignoring George Washington's admonition about being drawn into alliances, U.S. leaders made solemn pledges to come to the aid of no fewer than forty-one friendly nations should conditions so warrant. In exchange, American diplomats secured similar promises from foreign leaders. Before the Korean War, a peacetime United States had ever been unaligned and relatively unarmed. Ever since, it has been armed and allied.

Not surprisingly, the most stark contrast between conditions prior to and after the war is found on the former battlefield, the Korean Peninsula. No small amount of that change must be ascribed to the tireless efforts of the wily and aged South Korean leader, President Syngman Rhee. The leader of the Republic of Korea extracted substantial rewards from the

Americans for his delayed and reluctant agreement to the July 1953 cease-fire. He insisted on a mutual security pact with the U.S. and guarantees that America would complete its planned expansion of the U.S.-equipped and U.S.-trained ROK Army. In view of the fact that the Communists would have a million-man force on the Peninsula at war's end, these two provisions were entirely understandable. But there was more. Rhee demanded a promise that the U.S. would consult with his government prior to the Geneva political talks and withdraw from them should no progress be secured in ninety days. Finally, Syngman Rhee obtained a vow that the U.S. would supply long-term economic aid to his destitute and war-torn country.

The United States kept all these promises and ironically, in so doing, possibly destroyed its chance to achieve its long-standing aim for Korea. Washington had failed to secure its original goal—a free, unified, and democratic Korea—and with each passing year, that prospect dims. The root cause of the war was unification. Southerners and northerners alike were desirous of unity but each, in turn, refused to accept a confederation forcibly imposed by the other. Although there have been negotiations between the two Koreas, the growing economic disparity between the two halves has created an increasingly insurmountable obstacle. North Korea's per capita income is only about $900 per year. On the other hand, with the help of substantial U.S. economic assistance during the 1950s through the 1970s, southerners have raised their average annual income from practically nothing to $7,200. Just to bring the economic level of the North to 60 percent that of the South would cost southerners $40 billion per year for ten years, about one-eighth of South Korea's entire annual economic output.

This enormous difference and one of the sinister reasons for it is hidden from northerners by Pyongyang's strict control of information and a constant stream of warlike propaganda. The relative disparity in population between the two Koreas has remained about the same since the 1950s. The numbers of people in both countries doubled, with the northerners remaining about half as numerous as southerners. But over the intervening years, there has been a dramatic reversal in the comparative sizes of the two armed forces. Despite the 100 percent population growth, the uniformed strength of the Republic of Korea is only about 7 percent above what existed at the war's end. However, the North has greatly expanded its armed forces, achieving a fivefold growth since 1953. This large force, over 1.1 million members, is about twice the strength of South Korea's uniformed might. Beyond doubt, a prime reason for the relative poverty in North Korea is the constant struggle to maintain a bloated military establishment. And many southerners are fully aware of the fact that the Peninsula's military imbalance is greater today than it was in 1950.

Although the United States kept its word to the South, some claim it failed to keep faith with a special group of northerners. In May of 1952 North Korean partisans operating under American control numbered some 22,000, and this figure was projected to reach 40,000. However, with a growing realization that the war would probably reach a negotiated end along the existing front, U.S. leaders made the decision to curtail the partisan program and plan for its transfer to ROK control. This was a bitter pill to swallow for many of the northerners who believed the U.S. was intent on liberating their homeland. By January 1, 1953, the numbers had shrunk to 20,000 and were still falling as many of the guerrillas were simply drifting away from their island bases. They had been paid by and were loyal to their American advisers and mentors but distrusted southerners. Several thousand are known to have melted into the crowds of Seoul, disappearing into the civilian population of South Korea. An undetermined number are believed to have returned by sea to a dubious future in their native land: North Korea. In the end only about 10,000 partisans were accepted into the ROK Army. An indication of how they were received might be gleaned by the nature of the instructions South Korean officials issued in February 1954 on the eve of the transfer:

"The induction of these partisans into the ROK Army must not be considered a routine operation. Special precautionary measures must be taken in view of their peculiar background, training, indoctrination, and experience in unorthodox warfare during three years of guerrilla operations. . . . Partisans must be dispersed as individuals throughout the ROK Army so that not more than five to seven are assigned to a company and they should not be from the same partisan group. . . . Initially, members of the partisan forces should not be assigned to ROK units in the rear areas where it would be easy to desert and join bandit groups."

Partisan commanders facing an uncertain future. On the eve of their incorporation into the ROK Army, in early 1954, these North Korean guerrilla leaders were about to bid goodbye to their American advisers and enter into a new, unpredictable future.

But while the United States might be accused of breaking faith with these northerners, it surely could not be reasonably charged with selling out others. Half the war, some fifteen months, was fought over the issue of repatriation. But for that sticking point, the negotiations could have easily been concluded in early 1952. For the Americans, that meant that they were fighting for the right of some of their former enemies, their captives, to avoid return to either Communist China or Communist North Korea at war's end. During this time, the U.N. suffered 125,000 casualties, a human cost that represented more than twice the 50,000 Communists desiring not to be repatriated. There are few, if any, more unselfish, principled examples in the long history of warfare.

Another remarkable aspect of this war was its initial, causative dispute. That argument between two generals, one Russian, the other American, turned on the definition of one word: "democratic." The Russian insisted that only those Koreans who had previously supported a Soviet-American compact could be called democratic and allowed to participate in founding a post–World War II Korean government. The American insisted on hearing all voices, even those who disagreed with the Soviet-American pact. To Lieutenant General John Hodge and the United States, it was a matter of principle.

Despite the importance of this war, it has all but been erased from the American memory. Throughout the United States there are thousands of memorials and statues honoring the fallen of America's many wars. Almost all of these celebrate the nation's sacrifices of the Civil War or the two world wars. In Washington the most visited war memorial is the Vietnam Memorial. In 1992, fully ten years after that stark, black monument was erected, there was still no national memorial dedicated to those Americans who fought the Korean War. Throughout the long and passionate debate about the 2,483 Americans reported missing in action in the Vietnam War, there was a strange, almost embarrassing silence about those U.S.

servicemen who were in a similar status immediately after their disappearance during the Korean War. Unlike the missing of the Vietnam War, Americans who vanished during the Korean War were quickly declared "presumed dead." Had these missing soldiers, sailors, and marines of the 1950s been treated as the Vietnam veterans, their numbers would have been about twice the missing of the later conflict. It is little wonder the U.S. veterans of Korea have long dubbed their conflict "the Forgotten War."

The Korean War remains America's most misunderstood and ill-analyzed conflict. Those who called it "the wrong war at the wrong place at the wrong time" failed to comprehend that the truly just wars are fought not because they are convenient, but because a failure to resist, a failure to fight, would be morally wrong. There are, quite simply, conditions worse than war. Those who claimed the war to be the only one America had ever lost failed to acknowledge the conflict's actual results. An aggressor had been deprived of his unlawful gains, had been severely punished, and had his own territory reduced. Those who saw the war as a waste failed to see the war in its true light. The Korean War was the hot and bloody opening campaign of a global struggle misnamed the Cold War. That forty-five-year-long struggle retained the vital characteristic of its first campaign to the victorious end. Both the Cold War and the Korean War were waged by the West on principles that proved more compelling, more worthy, and more enduring than those of its adversary. For the United States, the Korean War was fought for the right reasons.

NOTES

Chapter 1:
Wrong Place, Wrong Time, Wrong War

The after-action report on the 1951 Wolfhound bayonet attack is taken from Operations Research Office, Johns Hopkins University, Far East Command, Technical Memorandum, "Notes on Infantry Tactics in Korea," by S.L.A. Marshall, February 28, 1951. Secretary of State Dean Acheson's remarks and the statement of the U.N. Commission on Korea are found in United States Mission to the United Nations, Department of State, "Transcript of a Statement by the Honorable Dean G. Acheson, Secretary of State, Before Committee I on the Korean Item" (New York, October 24, 1952). The exchange of letters between Lieutenant General Hodge and Colonel General Christiakov and the comment by Secretary of State George C. Marshall are taken from U.S. Department of State, "Korea's Independence" (Washington, D.C.: U.S. Government Printing Office, 1947), pp. 20–35. The comments of the two anti-Communist North Koreans come from U.S. Army Forces Far East, Military History Section, "U.N. Partisan Forces in the Korean Conflict" (Tokyo, March 1954), pp. 73–127. Statements from North Korean captives are taken from International

205

Public Opinion Research, Inc., revised by William Kendall, Operations Research Office, "Beliefs of Enemy Soldiers About the Korean War" (Tokyo, May 1952). The transcript of Radio Pyongyang's September 7, 1948, broadcast is taken from Headquarters, XXIV Corps, Assistant Chief of Staff, G-2, "Radio Intercepts" dated September 16, 1948, found in the Albert E. Brown papers, U.S. Army Military History Institute (MHI) Archives. Lieutenant Colonel Appleman's analysis is taken from his draft manuscript, "Korean Combat History," Volume I, Chapter III, MHI Document Collection. Information on the CIA station in Manchuria is taken from John K. Singlaub's oral history in the MHI Archives. CIA officer Jay D. Vanderpool's story of the faulty estimate of North Korean strength is from his oral history, p. 136, in the MHI Archives. President Truman's remarks are taken from his memoirs, *Years of Trial and Hope: 1946–1952* (New York: Signet Books, 1965), p. 377.

Chapter 2:
"Sir, We Got Company"

The story of the first days of the North Korean invasion including General MacArthur's report to the JCS is taken from the Appleman manuscript. Secretary of Defense Johnson's testimony is recorded in the U.S. Senate, 82nd Congress, First Session, Committee on Armed Services and Committee on Foreign Relations, "Hearings on the Facts Surrounding the Relief of General of the Army Douglas MacArthur" (hereinafter referred to as the MacArthur Hearings). The statements of the North Korean armor officers is taken from Operations Research Office, Johns Hopkins University, "The Employment of Armor in Korea," April 8, 1951, MHI Document Collection. The story of the 24th Infantry Division's misadventure is taken from Captain Russell A. Gugeler, *Combat Actions in Korea* (Washington, D.C.: U.S. Government Printing Office, 1953), pp. 3–19. General MacArthur's summary of the action up to the defense of the Pusan Perimeter is quoted from U.S. Department of State, "Action in Korea Under Unified Command: First Report to the Security Council by the United States Government" (Washington, D.C., July 25, 1950), pp. 6–7.

Chapter 3:
"Home by Thanksgiving"

Lieutenant Colonel Scherer's tale of integrating ROK soldiers into the 7th U.S. Infantry Division, Lieutenant Strickland's story of filming marines in Seoul and Major James W. Spellman's sad tale of supplying the 24th Division are taken from Captain John G. Westover's *Combat Support in Korea* (Washington, D.C.: Center of Military History, 1987), pp. 104–6 and 184–88. President Truman's report on his Wake Island meeting with General MacArthur and Ambassador Warren Austin's report to the Secretary General are recorded in U.S. Department of State, "United States Policy in the Korean Conflict, July 1950–February 1951" (Washington, D.C.: USGPO, 1951), pp. 19–22. The report of what General MacArthur told President Truman about the probability and consequences of Chinese Communist intervention in the war is found in the MacArthur Hearings, Part III, p. 1835. Kim Chang Song was interviewed by Major B. C. Mossman on November 4, 1952, on an island off the North Korean coast. The interview and the story of Kim's effort to liberate his home area from Communist rule are found in U.S. Army Far East, Military History Section, "U.N. Partisan Forces in the Korean Conflict, 1951–1952" (Tokyo, March 1954), pp. 87–93, MHI Document Collection.

Chapter 4:
Defeat of the U.N. Army

William Pounder's story about the failure to properly clothe American soldiers for the coming winter and Lieutenant Colonel Baker's tale of repairing tanks for the 25th Infantry Division are taken from Captain John G. Westover's *Combat Support in Korea* (Washington, D.C.: Center of Military History, 1987), pp. 171–75 and 128 respectively. Captain Martin Blumenson's story from interviews with the survivors of the 32nd Infantry's ordeal of November–December 1950 is found in Captain Russell A. Gugeler, *Combat Actions in Korea* (Washington, D.C.: U.S. Government Printing Office, 1953), pp. 62–87. President Truman's speech to the nation is recorded in U.S.

Department of State, "United States Policy in the Korean Conflict, July 1950–February 1951" (Washington, D.C., 1951), pp. 19–20.

Chapter 5:
Matthew B. Ridgway and the Renaissance

General Ridgway's commentary and that of Brigadier General Walter F. Winton are taken from two oral histories and a transcript of a seminar. These are found among the Ridgway papers at the U.S. Army Military History Institute Archives. See the August 29, 1969, interview between General Ridgway and Major Matthew P. Caulfield, USMC; the April 18, 1984, interview conducted by Dr. Maurice Matloff; and the May 9, 1984, transcript of the seminar held at Fort Leavenworth, Kansas. The latter transcript contains Brigadier General Winton's reflections. The comments of Sergeant (now Colonel) Harry G. Summers, Jr., were taken from his remarks at the U.S. Marine Corps Russell Leadership Conference, Quantico, Virginia, on the evening of April 14, 1994. The excerpt from the January 8, 1951, State of the Union address by President Truman, the January 17, 1951, statement by Secretary of State Acheson, and the full text of the Chinese reply are found in U.S. Department of State, "United States Policy in the Korean Conflict, July 1950–February 1951" (Washington, D.C., 1951), pp. 32, 33–34, and 35–36 respectively. The story of Task Force Crombez comes from the Blumenson interviews and research in Captain Russell A. Gugeler, *Combat Actions in Korea* (Washington, D.C.: U.S. Government Printing Office, 1953), pp. 134–36. Guerrilla leader Kim Yong Bok's account is from U.S. Army Far East, Military History Section, "U.N. Partisan Forces in the Korean Conflict, 1951–1952" (Tokyo, March 1954), pp. 116–17, MHI Document Collection.

Chapter 6:
Punch and Counterpunch

The comments about the firing of General MacArthur offered by General Ridgway are taken from pages 14–15 of the 1984 Matloff interview and are found in the Ridgway papers at the Military History

Institute. The story of the fighting withdrawal of the 7th Infantry in the face of the April 1951 Chinese offensive was gathered by Captain Russell A. Gugeler through interviews, examination of the terrain, and a study of battle reports. Gugeler's account is contained in the revised edition of *Combat Actions in Korea* (Washington, D.C.: U.S. Government Printing Office, 1970), pp. 144–53. The prisoner interrogation revealing Chinese reactions to U.S. air interdiction efforts is one of many taken from Operations Research Office, Far East Command, "A Study of the Effectiveness of Air Support Operations in Korea" (Tokyo, November 1951), pp. 2–9. General Partridge's acknowledgment of the ineffectiveness of American air operations at night, the quote from Lieutenant General Nam Il, and the story of the September 1951 MiG surge are found in Lieutenant Colonel Robert F. Futrell's *The United States Air Force in Korea, 1950–1953,* rev. ed. (Washington, D.C.: Office of Air Force History, 1983), pp. 325, 372, 403–5. General Vandenberg's hopes for Operation Strangle and the October 1951 description of the 38th Infantry's fighting in the Punchbowl area were published in United States Military Academy, "Operations in Korea" (West Point, N.Y., 1956), pp. 46–47 and 44–45 respectively. The May 21, 1951, debriefing of Captain James Jabara was transcribed from a tape, number 648, held in the U.S. Air Force Oral History Collection, United States Air Force Historical Research Center, Maxwell Air Force Base, Alabama. Secretary of State Dean Acheson's remarks on the steps leading to negotiations are taken from United States Mission to the United Nations, Department of State, "Transcript of a Statement by the Honorable Dean G. Acheson, Secretary of State, Before Committee I on the Korean Item" (New York, October 24, 1952), pp. 20–22. The continuation of guerrilla leader Kim Yong Bok's story is from U.S. Army Far East, Military History Section, "U.N. Partisan Forces in the Korean Conflict, 1951–1952" (Tokyo, March 1954), pp. 119–21, MHI Document Collection. General Momyer's characterization of the "North Korean" Air Force and the restrictions imposed on the American airmen by the Chinese sanctuary are from his book *Airpower in Three Wars* (Washington, D.C.: U.S. Government Printing Office, 1978), pp. 114–15.

Chapter 7:
Talk-Fight, Fight-Talk

The description of the lackluster progress of the truce talks and the impasse over the repatriation issue is from Secretary of State Acheson's presentation, United States Mission to the United Nations, Department of State, "Transcript of a Statement by the Honorable Dean G. Acheson, Secretary of State, Before Committee I on the Korean Item" (New York, October 24, 1952), pp. 22–23 and 24–27. The sad tale of Outpost Eerie is found in Captain Russell A. Gugeler, *Combat Actions in Korea* (Washington, D.C.: U.S. Government Printing Office, 1970), pp. 144–53. The description of rations, clothing, and showers is from Captain John G. Westover's *Combat Support in Korea* (Washington, D.C.: Center of Military History, 1987), pp. 162–64 and 177–78. The quotes from the South Korean prisoner of war camp officer and the Chinese prisoner are from a U.S. Army-sponsored study of the subject: Samuel M. Meyers and William C. Bradbury, "The Political Behavior of Korean and Chinese Prisoners of War in the Korean Conflict: A Historical Analysis" (Washington, D.C.: Human Resources Research Office, George Washington University, 1958), pp. 62–70. The description of the ROKA training and enhancement programs is taken from Major Robert K. Sawyer, revised by Dr. Walter G. Hermes, *KMAG in Peace and War* (Washington, D.C.: Center of Military History, 1988), pp. 179–84. The story of the valiant October 1952 defense of White Horse Hill by the ROK 9th Division is from Walter G. Hermes, *Truce Tent and Fighting Front* (Washington, D.C.: Office of the Chief of Military History, 1966), pp. 305–6.

Chapter 8:
A Truce of Sorts

The transcript of General Van Fleet's testimony is taken from U.S. Congress, House of Representatives, Committee on Armed Services, Hearings (Washington, D.C., March 4, 1953). Lieutenant General Nam Il's statement of April 9, 1953, the condition of Communist prisoners and the expenditure of artillery ammunition by the Communist side during the last months of the war, and President Eisenhower's reaction to the June 18 ROK-inspired prison break are found in Walter G. Hermes, *Truce Tent and Fighting Front* (Washington, D.C.: Office of the Chief of Military History, 1966), pp. 419, 451–58, 477–78. The stories of Captain Gerald Fink and the description of conditions in the Chinese prisoner of war camp at Kanggye are from Major James A. MacDonald, Jr., "The Problems of U.S. Marine Corps Prisoners of War in Korea" (Washington, D.C.: History and Museums Division, Headquarters, U.S. Marine Corps, 1988), pp. 60–69, 114–22. A summary of the reports concerning Communist war crimes during the Korean War is in Judge Advocate Section, Korean Communications Zone, "Interim Historical Report," June 30, 1953. The specific atrocities cited are found on pages 24 and 33. The U.S. Air Force "turkey shoot" of 1953 is described in Lieutenant Colonel Robert F. Futrell's *The United States Air Force in Korea, 1950–1953*, rev. ed. (Washington, D.C.: Office of Air Force History, 1983), pp. 652–57. First Lieutenant (now Colonel) Robert Gerard's recollections of the war's last day were given to the author on July 29, 1994.

Chapter 9:
The Meaning of It All

The analysis of the postwar controversy and its impact on the Department of Defense is from Doris M. Condit, *History of the Office of the Secretary of Defense: The Test of War: 1950–1953* (Washington, D.C.: Office of the Secretary of Defense, 1988), p. 537. The congressional testimony containing the views of Generals Clark, Van Fleet, and Stratemeyer and Admiral Joy is from U.S. Senate, Committee on the Judiciary, Subcommittee to Investigate the Administration of the Internal Security Act and Other Internal Security Laws, 84th Congress (Washington, D.C.: U.S. Government Printing Office, 1955), pp. 7–23. The January 1954 quotation from Secretary Dulles is found in Lieutenant Colonel Robert F. Futrell's *The United States Air Force in Korea, 1950–1953*, rev. ed. (Washington, D.C.: Office of Air Force History, 1983), p. 687. The U.N. participants' warning of an expanded war should it be resumed is from Walter G. Hermes, *Truce Tent and Fighting Front* (Washington, D.C.: Office of the Chief of Military History, 1966), p. 492. Air Force General William W. Momyer's description of postwar interservice strategy disputes is from his *Airpower in Three Wars* (Washington, D.C.: U.S. Government Printing Office, 1978), p. 6. Cost estimates for the reunification of the two Koreas are from the director of policy studies at the Research Institute for National Unification in Seoul, Kil Jeong Woo, as quoted by Andrew Pollack, "Unifying? Not Now, Please," *The New York Times* (July 24, 1994), p. E3. The fate of the U.S.-directed North Korean partisans is found in Operations Research Office, "U.N. Partisan Warfare in Korea, 1951–1954" (Washington, D.C.: Johns Hopkins University, 1956), pp. 140–43.